THE SEARCH FOR THE HOLY

THE SEARCH FOR THE HOLY

THE SEARCH
FOR THE HOLY

by William F. Kraft

THE WESTMINSTER PRESS

Philadelphia

ISBN 0-664-24923-X
LIBRARY OF CONGRESS CATALOG CARD NO. 72-152336

PUBLISHED BY THE WESTMINSTER PRESS ®
PHILADELPHIA, PENNSYLVANIA

PRINTED IN THE UNITED STATES OF AMERICA

For Patty

Contents

Preface

MY REASON for writing this book has its origin in my ambiguous feelings and questions about the meaning of God. Theories and explanations of the holy experience support both the idea of a Supreme Being and the idea that God is a projection of man himself. Both of these ideas are difficult to relate to—for me and, I believe, for many others. I want to experience a God whose impact on my life is both significant and lasting.

This yearning to experience a God often emerges, for example, in psychotherapy. I find that many people who are fighting unconscious conflicts are also desperately trying to make sense of their lives. Their loneliness, depression, anxiety, and frustration repeatedly manifest an absence of a basic presence. I see many others struggling to find a reason for being, and although many are successful and affluent, most of them are leading adequate, but meaningless, lives. They are normal in the ordinary, accepted sense of normalcy. I am convinced, however, that they are not what they realistically could be. Their lives are adjusted—accommodated—but are not really happy and meaningful.

I listen to these people in therapy, in groups, in classrooms, in hospitals, and in everyday encounters. I discover that embedded in these struggling personalities is a crucial search for an experience that would make all other experiences at least understandable. I also discover that some emerge from their apparently meaningless experiences to realize a deep and lasting meaning.

Numerous experiences in this realm evoked in me a desire for more research based on these kinds of questions: What is the meaning of this struggle? Is this pain simply a symptom of maladjustment, or can it be an indication of growth? Where and how do I find meaning that makes sense—even of apparent non-sense? Is this an experience of the Holy? If so, how and why does the holy experience occur? How and why does it not occur? What difference does it make? These are some of the questions I will investigate thoroughly and hope to answer in the following pages. My professional bias will be psychology, and my approach will be primarily phenomenological-existential.

Before I proceed with these investigations, I should like to thank some of the people who assisted me. Particular gratitude is due to Adrian van Kaam, my mentor, and to Bernard Boelen and Bert van Croonenberg for their personal and professional concern. I am also grateful to Regis Ebner and Clare McKeever for their editorial comments and to Lila Gould and Sylvia Lencyzk for their secretarial assistance. Finally, I thank my parents, on whose shoulders I stand, and my wife for her constructive criticism and supportive love.

W.F.K.

THE SEARCH FOR THE HOLY

THE SEARCH FOR THE HOLY

1
A Theory of Self

TO APPRECIATE my experience of the Holy I must understand myself. The search for God is also a search for man and the search for man includes the discovery of God. This re-search begins with man.

THE SELF

I, being man, interact in many ways. My most intimate and fulfilling interaction is my self presence to reality. For example, my self experience of a sunset differs radically from an everyday and work experience of a sunset. Usually I take a sunset for granted, or I may curiously analyze it. In my self dimension, however, I experience an uncanny feeling of being one with the sunset—in a sense I am the sunset. I do little, if any, thinking in my purest moments; my experience automatically excludes rational analysis in favor of intimacy and self surrender. In this beautiful encounter I am willing to obey and follow the mystery of reality, and in my awesome reverence I experience a certain kinship with nature. Although I am totally involved, I know intuitively that I am most uniquely me, that my own singularity stands out in clear relief.

This self experience also incorporates a mysterious and paradoxical encounter with the sunset wherein I am able to experience joy and dread, to be proud and humble, to feel freely dependent, and to feel significantly insignificant. I may feel confident and strong, free and independent, yet I may also feel very small. I may also experience myself as being out of my body and yet one with my body. I experience myself as being one with the universe and as a very limited part of an unlimited whole.

My self experience also includes a concrete and ecstatic transcendence. This does not mean that I escape into fantasy, but that I experience reality in a different way. I move beyond my usual modes of interaction and I surrender myself to a reality that is more than me. In this transcendent encounter I feel that I am one with the sunset. Even though I may have many problems, my transcendence enables me to experience the fundamental unity in life, and in this way, I go beyond my limits. Transcendence offers me a richer appreciation of life that can even bring new meaning to the limits of everyday living. I experience my limits as being part of living and as a challenging avenue to its deeper dimensions.

Another way to look at a person as self is in terms of his interpersonal relationships. I as self have a respectful reverence for another person. I have the propensity to give to, and to be one with, him. I have no need to manipulate or dominate him, nor do I need to seduce him to satisfy my own needs. I am not seduced by his sensuality, nor do I analyze him. In my self dimension I take a second look at, or respect, the uniqueness of him. I feel a spontaneous and centrifugal inclination to accept, affirm, and understand this person.

In love, the most fundamental and highest form of self interaction, I reveal and offer the most intimate dimension of my being—my self. I am most uniquely and personally me in love. I take off my everyday masks to be myself-for-the-other. I paradoxically feel most myself in the very act of giving myself, and I begin to see differently because new possibilities emerge on my horizon of love. In love I give myself to and for the other's sake, for I desire to promote his happiness and welfare. My availability-for-the-other is end-centered in that it is a pure giving and not a means toward another end. In love I give myself unconditionally. I love a person for what and who he is. My love does not depend on how he behaves.

In love I also reveal my most vulnerable aspect— my self. Although I gain my deepest strength in love, the pain received in love is most penetrating. Thus, when I am hurt in love I may be very reluctant to reveal myself again, or I may look for certain guarantees that I will not be hurt again. Unfortunately, some people may go through their lifetimes seeking these guarantees and consequently never risking themselves in love. If everyone is waiting for the guarantee of not being hurt, then no one may extend the risky invitation to another in love. Thus, we arrive at the tragic situation wherein a person lives and dies with the frustrating wish that someone else will take the first step. A lover, who is willing to suffer for the other's sake, finds that pain in love makes sense.

My self dimension is also critical for my intrapersonal life. For instance, my most fundamental and long-range decisions are usually a result of my "transrational" self processes, not a result of a conscious, planned, and analytical process. In my self dimension, I opt for basic orientation—to be open or closed toward significant experiences or situations. When a person falls in love, he does not systematically gather knowledge about his possible beloved, analyze the data, and then decide whether or not to love her. Love is not this cold and calculating. On the contrary, love transcends rational analysis to a level of self surrender. Love is a mysterious happening. A person finds himself in love; he does not put himself in love. His decision is not to like this or that attribute of another, but he sees these qualities in the light of love. His self decision of love enables him to love himself and the other regardless of desirable or undesirable attributes.

A person whose main motivation comes from his self lives an orientation of openness and love. He becomes a dynamic discoverer who is constantly uncovering reality and growing into its mystery. He becomes more and more in tune with reality by openly admitting his experiences. His option to make discovery his life project means that he grows in the celebration of life. In the following analyses we will consider some significant experiences and functions of a person who lives primarily according to his self.

Authority and Obedience

In my self dimension, I experience an inner freedom and responsibility wherein I am the author and origin of my acts. I experience my most fundamental authority. Self authority comes from within me and serves as the basis of the various kinds of authority that I receive from my functions in life. The authority I *am* acts as the foundation for the authority I *have*. For example, if a teacher is not the authentic author of his life, his role authority will be an intrusive technique that elicits disrespect and resentment. His functional authority, without personal authority, will breed discontent. Fundamentally, a *person,* not a role, commands respect and obedience.

Paradoxically, personal authority is achieved primarily through obedience to myself and the Other. (Here the term "Other" refers to man and the Holy.) Obedience means to listen to the sense in a situation. When I listen I can begin to discover the truth. True obedience must begin with myself, and when I can listen to my own truth, the truth of the Other will begin to resonate within me. Thus, I can be truly obedient to others only if I am obedient to myself. My obedience will liberate me at least in becoming more sensitive in differentiating truth from fiction. Too often, however, I hear only what I want to hear. I hear only what fits into my frames of reference. For example, when someone tells me something I am inclined to accept only those views which support my own. To listen openly means that I must temporarily suspend my own point of view in favor of the other person's viewpoint. Only then can I understand what the person is really saying. The art of obeying involves the ability to shut up and really listen to what is being said.

Obedience and authority are mutually implicated. The true authority obeys and acts on the sense in himself and in others. The more he listens, the more he is capable of making a good decision. Furthermore, his respectful listening will appeal to others to listen to and consequently obey him. Likewise, the truly obedient person learns to be the author of his existence. His listening helps him to determine himself by opening him to the emergence of reality. He becomes an authority on living his life by listening to it.

Autonomy

Although autonomy is not the exclusive domain of the self, it is another of its important functions. The etymology of autonomy—the Greek *autos* (same, self) and *nomos* (law)—points to the fundamental reality of autonomy. An autonomous person lives according to internal convictions. His "laws" are in tune with himself. When I authentically actualize myself, the main motivating force of my life comes from within. I realize that although I depend on others, only I can live my life. Yet, my autonomy also means that I can freely choose to be dependent.

My self independency also enables me to transcend many everyday problems and to discover deeper meaning in reality. I am not so conditioned by the environment that I react automatically, but I am free to experience many meanings in the same situation. For example, a person's hostility does not automatically evoke hostility in me. His hostility may mean that he is hurt or frightened, that I am hostile toward him, that he learned to be hostile to survive, or that, most of all, he hates himself.

Freedom

We can also consider freedom to be primarily a function of the self in several ways. First, the most fundamental form of freedom is *freedom-to-be,* or self determination. As a free person I determine my life insofar as my openness enables me to say yes or no to realities. My freedom-to-be also means that since I commit myself to grow progressively deeper into reality, my field of possibilities expands; I experience more possibilities in my situation. My liberating growth demands commitment, for my life necessitates that I be in tune with and promote the Other. I *must* be open and caring in order to be free.

Freedom also implies a lack of restraint, and in this sense freedom is a *freedom-from.* Determining myself, I am unlikely to be seduced by the immediacy of the world. I am not completely bound by my situation. Although my environment may offer me few opportunities, I am free to transcend and acquire deeper meaning in my constricted environment. For example, a "free" prisoner might find deeper meaning in a concentration camp than a person imprisoned in opulence.

Furthermore, my freedom is limited. For instance, my decision for something excludes many other things. A person who opts for celibacy cannot be the same witness to marriage as can the married person, an option to live in the United States excludes living in Europe, and an option to love precludes hate. The limits of my body or the body-at-large—the world—are also incorporated in freedom. Since my freedom is embodied, I am never completely free. However, being free, I am well aware of my limits, and my knowledge helps me to transcend them.

Being limited, my freedom calls for discipline. I am disciplined when I am a disciple or follower of reality. My disciplined presence to reality enables me to admit what is happening; I can freely say yes or no to my experience. For example, when I can be open to my unwanted inclinations, not only am I liberating myself from the immature or unhealthy shackles of repression but I also gain a creative control and sense of my desires. This is discipline and freedom.

My freedom also influences my everyday behavior. I am able to "express" and to share myself in a more flexible and disciplined way. My thinking also becomes more flexible. I am free enough to consider many points of view, and am not bound merely by my own viewpoint. I become an inner-directed man who is a witness to a free life.

Faith

Faith is essentially linked with acceptance. When I opt to be open to my experience, I accept (*ad-*

cipere = to take in) or admit (*ad-mittere* = to send toward) my experiences. It can be said that I "own up to them." When I admit (to) my experiences I affirm them and "let them in" to my being. Acceptance also promotes responsibility in that I am able to respond to situations more openly.

In this psychological context we define faith as a creative acceptance or admittance of experiences that cannot be explained. Although some of my experiences are inexplicable, they are nevertheless real and are known by me prereflectively. My faith involves a dynamic and affirmative incorporation of the mystery of reality. My faith is not speculation wherein I reflect on the possibilities of a situation. Neither is my faith a type of magical thinking wherein I make reality be what I want it to be, nor is my faith a rationalization used to justify something that I do not experience. My faith is an affirmation and incorporation of my experience, not a means of reinforcing fantasy.

My faith is always and necessarily faith *in* something, because my faith is a response (of acceptance) to a call of reality. This appeal from reality is not faith, but faith is my open response to the mystery of reality. Thus, the main impetus of faith comes from within me. In faith I accept (faith) or reject (bad faith) my experience. When I opt to accept the mystery of life, I affirm and validate my experience. Furthermore, my yes to reality incorporates a commitment to what I have faith in. Faith means that I will continue to follow reality and consequently become a disciple of mystery.

I have faith not only in the Other but also in myself. Much of my experience cannot be explained but should be accepted. To be healthy I must promote a dynamic presence to my own experience, for without this faith in myself I will know almost nothing. Finally, faith in myself is a necessary condition for faith in another. I must accept that which I experience before I can accept that which another experiences. How can I accept the mystery of another if I am not open to my own mystery?

Gordon Allport states that a person who is authentically faithful must come to a "heuristic belief" —one that is never absolutely sure but grows in degrees of probability. (*The Individual and His Religion,* pp. 72–74.) Although an absolute faith may give a temporary sense of false security in knowing all the answers, this faith robs reality of its mystery and will eventually disintegrate. Absolute certainty is, moreover, inauthentic and impossible because it is against the emergent nature of reality. Authentic faith is a matter of personal development, not a matter of having a method to justify the unknown. A faithful person grows in degrees of certitude and progressively opens up to new horizons.

We can see that faith and openness are dialectically related. Faith presupposes the option of openness because I can only accept the mystery that I am open to, and my faith moves me to accept and witness to that mystery. If I do not affirm and incorporate mystery, my openness will become a fantasy. Thus, a faithful person is open to and is a living witness to the mystery of reality.

THE EGO

My ego mode of existence is oriented to the worlds of work, science, and task-oriented behavior in general. For example, most workers must be relatively impersonal in contrast to their more personal self modes of interaction. Think of how a businessman behaves in his work situation; his behavior is mainly task-oriented. He has a job to do and his main concern is to come to grips with the demands of his task in a practical and efficient way. His business life usually demands that he think and act in a purposeful and logical way. Since management, organization, and control are important, he often operates on a quasi-scientific and technical level. He is constantly solving "problems"—issues that must be settled or proved true or false.

The surgeon, for example, is necessarily task-oriented and impersonal in his surgery. Purely personal behavior would be inappropriate. The surgeon must be exact and precise in the technique of his profession. He should know, as much as humanly possible, what is and will occur; he must be in control of the situation. Although a patient wants to be treated with personal care in the pre- and post-operative periods, he would be incensed if the surgeon would take a personal therapeutic approach during the operation. The patient expects that the surgeon will be cold, efficient, and manipulative while operating on him.

Or, it is absurd for a plumber to be personally intimate when repairing a clogged drain. It is equally ridiculous for a mother to maintain a playful attitude when her child gets hurt. She must take charge, put her feelings aside, size up the situation, and act to solve the problem. Her behavior may be motivated by and permeated with love, but her actions to help her child must be efficient and task-oriented.

We can see that in my ego interaction I take a conscious distance from a situation, which makes for clear thinking and impersonal involvement. My ego presence to reality is precise and definitive. It is not immediate, private, or impulsive as the interaction of my body, nor is it paradoxical, ineffable, direct, and universal as my self presence, but my ego interaction is clear, mediate, public, and abstract. My ego presence is also oriented to the common world—the world of common discourse. For example, when I use ego language I am exposing myself to the public and am inviting criticism. Most ego language is open to all; it is not intimate or private. Public systems of communication, especially verbal speech, depend on ego processes, and without the ego, nothing could be written, built, or verbally spoken. In short, in my ego dimension I deal more with the clear and public as contrasted with the paradoxical and unique of the self.

My ego functions primarily in terms of reflective thinking and willing. I reflect rationally on a situation, think about it, and then make a decision. I attack reality in terms of a problem-solving situation and I am in control of what I am doing. However, a difficulty arises when I reflect on my experience, because my experience can never be exactly reflected or thought out in exact terms. My immediate experience is always more than my mediated ego knowledge. Even though ego communication is always inadequate, especially with intimate experiences, it is very valuable and necessary. Ego discourse promotes explicit sharing of experiences, as in speaking and writing, and it enables me to gain more control, clarification, and insight into my experience.

Man as ego can be considered to be manager. Every person is a manager in some area of his intra- and extra-psychic life. A housewife must manage her household chores; the businessman manages his work and personnel; the father must manage the finances; the student must manage his studies. A person must also manage to act appropriately in situations, manage to think correctly, manage space and time, manage to make sense, and manage himself. Management connotes control of a situation as a means of meeting certain goals wherein I manage to organize reality in a task-oriented manner. I more or less calculate, plan, and consciously put things into place. For instance, I reflect on my feelings, moods, thoughts, and standards, and try to make explicit sense of them. The numerous demands and possibilities of my world must also be put in order; otherwise, my life becomes a chaos. Finally, I strive for a balanced integration between the internal and the external dimensions of my life.

In an ego mode of existence I am capable of detaching myself from a situation to protect myself or to take a second look at myself. I am not likely to follow blindly the loudest and most articulate voice. Neither will I be prone to be seduced by group hysteria. Nor will I tend to act impulsively when under pressure. By dealing with and coping with the situation at hand, I do not become inappropriately involved, but I realistically meet the demands of my situation.

Finally, my ego enables me to practice what I preach. My creative self insights remain in my mind and do not affect the world unless they are implemented by my ego. Ideas may come easily, but the execution of ideas takes much ego work in the forms of thinking, decision-making, planning, analyzing, organizing, and problem-solving. Ideally, I should strive for a harmony between my self and ego processes. Without the creativity of my self, my ego functions become useless means and frequently become ends in themselves, and I soon become an efficient barbarian. Without the functions of my ego, my self becomes a seductive fantasy often resulting in a schizoid mode of living.

THE BODY

Man's psychological body refers to his third primary presence to reality—the body that interacts in the world with others. This body is not the body of medicine, physiology, or biochemistry; it is my body which I live. My lived-body also has distinctive functions which differ from those of my ego and self. For instance, a person who drives an automobile usually does not think to increase speed, brake, steer, or find

directions. He trusts his prereflective knowledge of
driving and seldom gives it a thought. He usually
thinks about his driving only if something goes
wrong. His body—hands, arms, legs, eyes, ears, etc.
—knows how to drive. If he had to reason every operation, the effort and tension would exhaust him
and impede the smooth flow of his driving. Neither
does this person have an intimate and transcendent
encounter, for such behavior would be simply inappropriate and probably would cause an accident.

Likewise, the fingers of the violinist know the con-
certo better than his ego. In fact, if during a per-
formance he were to take time to reflect, his music
would become noise. The fingers of the typist also
know the keys better than her ego, so that when the
typist begins to think, she usually makes mistakes or
slows up. In the same way the athlete cannot afford
to think when playing the game. This is what time-
outs are for. Finally, a person's spontaneous body
knowledge and language in sexuality may be truer
and less inhibiting than those of his ego. When a
person begins to think in sexual dialogue he becomes
once removed from the situation. The ultimate of
sexuality is to let myself know the other without
the impurities of thinking.

My bodily interaction with reality is immediate
and prereflective, and my knowledge is, at least initially, implicit and undifferentiated. For example,
my bodily feelings seldom lie, for they are in direct
and pure contact with the world. However, the
knowledge of my feelings is ambiguous and equiv-
ocal and it tends to intermingle with the knowledge

of my other feelings. It behooves me to be openly present to the messages of my body and then periodically to think about them. This thinking is important because it enables my ambiguous body knowledge to become clear and distinct. I must remember, however, that (ego) thinking about my feelings is fruitless without a prior and necessary (self) openness to them.

Rooting me in the world and anchoring me to the earth, my body draws the world into me. For instance, my senses bring the world to me in their various modalities. Since I and another necessarily express ourselves in and through our bodies, we can know each other. My body makes me and another present and accessible to each other. Without my body, I am no-where, no-one, and no-body.

The density and demands of my body are also constant reminders of my embeddedness in the world. My body prevents me from living exclusively in a mental world. Because I am an embodied person, I must live the fundamental structures of reality. I must eat, sleep, be sheltered, live in time and space, and contact the world through the structures of my senses and nervous system. If I abuse these structures, I will pay the price. If I eat too much, I get fat. If I do not eat enough, I become weak. If I refuse to follow these rules, I will die physically or psychologically. Indeed, although I must obey these rules, I am marginally free in regard to their particular execution.

I—as embodied psyche—am also structured in that I can make contact only through perspective.

My bodily modalities of the senses, movements, and postures let me see the world in and through perspective, and consequently I can reach the Other only in limited ways. Even though my self enables me to be a horizon of possibilities, my body forces me to actualize only a few of them.

Finally, my body is impulsive and selfish without the mediative thought of my ego or the respect of my self. My body in itself strives for immediate relief and will blindly use anything or anybody to achieve its pleasure. This kind of bodily existence is exclusive of the Other in that it acts only on behalf of its own interests. Although my body puts me in the world and enables me to contact the Other, my body needs my ego and my self to become truly human.

Conclusions

Everyday Behavior

My usual or everyday behavior normally calls for body and/or ego modes of interaction, while my self is not directly expressed. For instance, a housewife's behavior does not usually call for self-interaction. Expression of her self while cleaning the house, changing diapers, or taking a coffee break would be inappropriate behavior. However, her self can be implicitly present or absent. If a housewife represses her self, her everyday behavior becomes merely functional and without significant purpose, resulting in boredom. If her self influences her everyday ego and body interaction, her routine will be permeated with

transcendent purpose. If her self is present and expressed explicitly in appropriate situations, her routine living and work will be made easier and more
meaningful. Her self experiences will have the effect
of liberating her in all modes of behavior—including
her work. Furthermore, if her everyday life should
change, as with the unexpected appearance of her
husband or with loving demands from her children,
she is ready to express herself overtly in love.

Such self experiences as love, however, have been
relegated to certain situations and to particular
times. This is usually valid, for a person cannot always be loving overtly. Love is too intense to be constantly explicit, and besides, most situations do not
call for such love. However, it is very important to
realize that a person can always express his love implicitly in that all his behavior can be performed in
the context of love. He can live with an orientation
of love. For example, a teacher who acts merely on
an ego level lacks conviction, and his students experience him as efficiently boring. He can also stand
out on an ego and bodily level, which he usually
must do, within the context of self spontaneity and
concern. Although he may express his self directly,
if it is appropriate, his self usually forms the background for the foreground of his body and ego functions. Pupils experience this teacher as a genuine,
open, and concerned educator. This situation is conducive to learning.

Likewise, the nurse who operates only on an ego
level is an efficient though poor nurse. Authentic
nursing incorporates both self and ego functions. A

nurse's self, although usually implicit, humanizes the nursing techniques. We can say that nursing techniques without concern are cold and make for efficient robots, but that techniques used in the context of love and as implementations of care make for warm and therapeutic nurses. Patients experience authentic nurses as trained persons who really care.

My body is also in tune with love at least insofar as I must "express" my love as a man or as a woman. My authentic love is always incarnated in this sexual way. However, romantic love is intensely embedded in the emotions and is therefore experienced as intensely real. Love expressed in genital sexuality explicitly incorporates both body and self, resulting in the unique unity of self transcendency and bodily pleasure.

Beauty

Beauty is a mode of behavior that involves a harmony of the self, ego, and body with the self as the main dynamic force. As in music, my transcendent joy and immediate pleasure are embedded within a certain framework—a framework that is bounded by ego technique. Thus, when I enjoy a symphony I experience a transcendent and pleasurable truth within the context of the musical framework and virtuosity. My experience of beauty in nature, such as of a sunset, is fundamentally the same as in an art work. Although the form or mode of expression is not made by man, the form still exists. Thus, in an aesthetic experience I enjoy letting my whole being be.

Play

One of the most interesting and fascinating kinds of behavior is play. A significant factor in play is that it incorporates certain structures and/or rules that safeguard me from being hurt. Since I and another know, consciously or unconsciously, the structure of our play situation, we can afford to be at ease. We do not have to hide or to be phony. Although my play is not usually as intimate as my love, I do experience a freedom to be myself with a minimum risk of being hurt.

Play is ordinarily an interpersonal relationship. Even when I play by myself, another is usually present in my fantasy. However, my main intention is not to give to the Other, as in love, but simply to express, which may involve giving. Thus, play is more a question of being and expression that bring a sense of well-being. We can simply be ourselves.

My play differs radically from my customary activity. I take time out from my everyday and work worlds to re-create and play. Since play is a creative retreat from my everyday worlds of tension, play is a pretension. It comes before and after the tension of ordinary living.

Any mode of presence can be accented in play. For example, a child's play is centered on his body and frequently serves as an avenue for his ego to explore reality. Sexual play allows a person to express directly through the immediacy of his body. Intellectual games offer his ego functions an added degree of free expression. Play in the self dimension is my deepest mode of dwelling-in and being-with the world. To play with another in love, to feast with friends, to dwell in nature, and to laugh at myself can all be modes of playful celebration.

Person and Personality

Finally, we can consider the terms "person" and "personality" in the light of our framework. The etymology of person means an actor's mask or a character in a play. Mask need not be used in the sense of hiding from the world, but used as a particular mode of facing the world. To be a person, one must interact in the self, ego, or bodily modes of presence. Thus, only man can be a person. An infant, for instance, is a person because he interacts with his environment, although explicitly only on a bodily level. A neurotic, who attempts to reject some of his experiences, is nevertheless a person because he is involved in the world, although in a relatively closed manner. Likewise, one who is mentally retarded is a person; the same is true for a psychotic person. Thus, all people—of all ages, degrees of health and intelligence, races, cultures, etc.—can and should be respected as persons.

We define personality as a dynamic gestalt of a person's actual modes of experience. Therefore, personality presupposes the person and is determined by the person and other factors, such as genetic endowment, environment, culture, temperament, and interpersonal relationships. A person's personality is always unique, for it incorporates the unique quality and degree of his body, ego, and self actualization. A child, for instance, has a personality, but it is not as matured as a healthy adult's. It may also be said that one person has a dynamic personality and another has a lethargic personality. However, since person and personality are not synonymous, a person may have a rather dead personality and still be a healthy person. On the other hand, a person may have a dynamic personality and be rather unhealthy. The healthy person, however, usually has an appealing and comforting personality.

2
Man's Experience of the Holy

MY RE-SEARCH for the holy experience took me in many directions. I read the literature on God. The mystics and spiritual writers offered me personal insights into the experience of God, and the scholars gave me reasons for and against the existence of God. In my work with small groups people frequently expressed a genuine concern for the relevance of God. Openly expressing ourselves, we found that each person's experience of God differed somewhat from another's. We realized that such factors as religion, ethnic background, constitution, personal history, education, and maturity influenced our experience of God. Nevertheless, we came to a common ground—a ground that made all our experiences holy.

I also asked people to write spontaneous descriptions about their experience of God. I had them describe a holy experience as openly as possible, without using theories about God. These naïve descriptions helped me to understand what people mean by a holy experience.

Finally, I listened to individuals in counseling and in friendly dialogue. I realized that although people used various terms in talking of this holy experience, such as God, Absolute Thou, Personal Transcendent, ultimate concern, and religious and mystical experience, all were pointing to the same reality. I also listened to my own holy experiences and tried to explicate what happened. The goal of the following analyses is to present the common factors of these direct and indirect experiences of the Holy while remaining faithful to each experience.

MYSTERY AND PARADOX

Like all my self experiences, my holy experience incorporates mystery and paradox. My mysterious encounter with the Holy points to an ineffable and unusual quality that transcends my normal behavior of ego problem-solving and immediate body satisfaction. Although my holy experience can be pointed to and described partially with words, usually best in poetic and mystical terms, my experience does not lend itself to exact communication. My knowledge of the Holy is so intimate and so beyond my everyday modes of interaction that it becomes extremely difficult to talk about this experience or to reason with it. I face a danger in attempting to become too exact in analyzing my holy experiences. Such certainty can lead to reification, sterilization, and a tendency toward falsification of my holy experience. On the other hand, I must remember that although my paradoxical holy experience is beyond the level of ego analysis, it nevertheless points to a lived and undeniable experience. A refusal to look at my holy experience could become a denial of my reality whether my denial is done in the name of scientism or spiritualism.

My self experiences of the Holy are also paradoxical, and consequently they seem contradictory or meaningless from a logical perspective. My paradoxical presence to the Holy is a-logical, a-contradictory, and a-discursive. My uncanny and strangely attractive experience is beyond my normal world of dichotomies, either/or, problems, analysis, and distances, for in my holy experience I surrender myself to unity, both/and, mystery, synthesis, and closeness. In my holy encounters I experience the unity of joy and anxiety, attraction and respectful distance, fascination and trepidation, familiarity and mystery, pride and humility. I realize immediately that my sacred experience is related integrally with the profane. My sacred stance becomes profane because I am more deeply in the world, and my profane stance becomes sacred because my world is made holy. Thus, in and through my holy transcendence, I spontaneously take up a new and deeper kinship with the world.

DEPENDENCE

My self experience of the Holy demands that I give myself to the Other. I depend on the Other because I need the Other to love the Other. In fact, although I need the Other to exist, my acceptance of this dependence makes me free and independent. To be a holy person means that I choose to promote the human and holy Other in my life and thereby gain a new independence and freedom.

I realize that since I cannot force the holy reality to reveal itself and to respond to me, I must depend on the Holy. However, although I can never force the Other to encounter me, I can take the initiative to be available when the Other reveals himself to me. I also acknowledge that the human and holy Other is a greater and holier reality than myself, and consequently I tend to give a spontaneous respect to the Other. I find that the Other is overwhelming in reference to me. I know that the human and holy Other is the ground of my existence and that only the Other can fill me with life. Thus, I slowly come to realize that my holy dependence means that the human and holy Other is the ground of my being. A denial of this condition means that I would lose my ground and progressively lead a meaningless life. Finally, I humbly acknowledge that the Holy also depends on me in that the Holy manifests itself most meaningfully in and through man. Without man the Holy does not exist for man, because man is the locus for the manifestation of the Holy.

My holy dependence differs radically from infantile, immature, and unhealthy modes of dependency. For instance, since an infant's mode of existence is a bodily one, it is necessary for the infant to take constantly and impossible for him to give willingly. Thus, if a person is immature or regressed, he acts in a way similar to the child. Similarly, an unhealthy dependent person centers his life around satisfying his own needs and not around giving to the Other. His dependency forces him to see life only in terms of his own needs. He may be concerned about the Other, but only for his own welfare and not for the Other's sake. If his needs are unsatisfied, he feels inferior, uneasy, and dependent. This person leads a precarious existence because he compulsively depends on dependency. He cannot choose freely to be authentically dependent on the Other. Often this person will put on a front of being independent because it proves to be an efficient way of satisfying his dependency needs without losing face. Or, he will simply be passively dependent, for most people like quiet and dependent persons in small doses. This person's unconscious exploitation of man and of the Holy makes his love a means only to receive love.

A holy and healthy person owns up to his dependency, a dependency that is centered around giving. Recognizing his need to love the Other, this person becomes dependable : he is available to the Other. He does not give to the Other in order to satisfy a deficiency, but he loves the human and holy Other for the Other's sake. It is the right thing to do.

INDEBTEDNESS

In love, I find that I have been thrown into the world with the vocation of being concerned for the Other. I admit that to be truly alive is to give, and I openly respond to this call. This call to give points

to a primordial mood of indebtedness. I feel that I
owe myself to the Other, and I realize that I can be a
person only with the Other.

I also realize that I have a large debt to pay because I owe the Other my existence. My debt is
rooted fundamentally in love at least insofar as my
parents, friends, and society have enabled me to become myself. Without their love and the acts emergent from their love, I could not have lived, let alone
developed into a person. I have been given so much,
especially in childhood, that I have a life debt to pay.
I acknowledge that every person is indebted to the
Other for his life and that life without the Other is a
fictive life.

Although my body and ego are indebted to others,
my primordial mood of indebtedness is oriented
around my self. My self indebtedness is more critical
to life than that of my ego and body. For example,
when I receive "something," I usually feel obliged to
return something else. If a thing symbolizes the gift
of another person, however, it makes the thing more
meaningful and personal. The most risky and intimate gift is of myself in love, for this gift calls for
the greatest giving, receiving, and returning. I cannot
replace this gift with things; I can only reciprocate
with the same gift—myself.

I realize that to give myself to the Other is my
most demanding and crucial debt. If I and others do
not return the gift of ourselves to each other, life
and society will degenerate. When people never give
of themselves, the culture suffers and becomes a culture of things, not of persons.

I pay my debt to the human and holy Other most

basically by loving the Other. The Other makes demands on me in terms of appeal, not force, because the Other simply asks nothing more than love. The purpose of paying my debt is not to receive a reward. That giving is business. If I should demand a return, I would make love a subtle means of personal satisfaction instead of a promotion of the Other. When I use love to get the rewards of wholeness and holiness, I pervert love and become less whole and holy. A true gift is a giving of myself without the demand of a return. Finally, I again come into the paradoxical realm in that the more I pay my debt, the more I am in debt, because the more I give to the Other, the more the Other returns to me. Thus, my degree of indebtedness is indicative of my degree of holiness.

At times I may experience a peculiar and subtle sense of guilt with my indebtedness. I feel a primordial unrest, an uncanny uneasiness that is never completely eased. My guilt means that I am in a state of not-yetness, that I am always becoming in my holy encounters. Yet, my guilt enables me to give more to the Other and consequently to be more of myself. Thus, to be a holy person means that I must live in guilt. I feel guilty in that I am returning so little compared to what I have received and am receiving. I feel that I am not living up to the call of the Other and that I am not actualizing my potential to be with the Other. My guilt does not stem from a compulsive attempt to be perfect—to be god—so that I suffer neurotic guilt when I am not 100 percent right. On the contrary, my guilt is a living affirmation of my humanity—that my life is unceasingly growing.

WORSHIP

Worship points to the ways in which I respect, affirm, and give to the Other. The primordial ground and highest form of worship is love. Although my indebtedness and guilt move me to worship, my primary aim is not to pay my debt or to relieve my guilt. I most authentically worship the Other because I love the Other. Without love, my worship becomes a childish and often meaningless ritual, and with love, my worship becomes a meaningful implementation of and witness to love. For instance, a mature husband worships his wife simply because she is worthy of worship. He does not make her a pseudo god so that his worship is fictive and egoistic, but his healthy worship means that he accepts and interacts with his wife as herself. He promotes her well-being, her wholeness and holiness, for he helps her to actualize herself in all dimensions, including her holy life. Thus my worship of man need not be idolatrous, because true worship incorporates in some way an encounter with the human and holy Other. I worship because I love; that is, the human and holy Other, being my ultimate concern in life, simply calls for worship.

My authentic worship is not one of a lower subject looking up at a higher subject. This was often the worship of antiquity. Neither do I worship to propitiate a powerful and primitive god. My encounter is not a submission of will. On the contrary, I freely realize that the Other is greater than myself and that the power of the Other is the inviting power of love. My worship is a yes to these realities. My worship also says that I am grateful to the Other for making me be, and I give thanks for this gift of life.

Finally, my worship can take many forms: formal and informal, verbal and nonverbal, private and public, and explicit and implicit. For example, I can learn meaningful forms of public worship that have an advantage of incorporating a communal aspect, wherein I can participate in the same form of worship as others, and thereby promote a personal communion with my fellowman. I must realize, however, that these types of worship are meaningless and a sham unless they are personalized by me. Furthermore, although these avenues of worshiping are very important, I must constantly try to discover new ways of worshiping the Other. For instance, I may discover that love is one of my purest forms of worship, or I may find that my everyday life, when lived in the context of love, becomes a subtle, yet ever-present worship of the Other.

FAITH AND DOUBT

Before, during, and after my holy encounters, I experience a paradoxical unity of faith and doubt. My faith incorporates doubt and my doubt incorporates faith. I find that my faith needs doubt in order to develop and that my doubt is the darkness that enables the light of faith to be seen.

We have already seen that the self function of faith is not a question of certainty or exactness but a question of mystery. In and through faith I openly and creatively accept my numinous experiences and thereby grow into the ground of reality. Although my experience is inexplicable, I must admit that I need faith in order to love, because love is beyond the control of the ego and body.

Likewise, I experience doubt in my holy experience in that I am questioning and growing closer to the Other. I am never certain of the Other. Certainty would mean that I know everything exactly and thus control everything. In fact, paradoxically, my lack of doubt would mean that I could not trust or risk being open to the mystery of the Other. Such a person lives a fictive life, because a life without doubt exists only in fantasy. Just as disastrous is the person who is in a chronic state of doubt. It is impossible for this person to accept the unsolvable in faith. However, the authentic person is always to some degree in doubt of the Other. At times, my doubt can become so great that I need faith to make sense out of my experience. At other times, I may achieve a high degree of enlightenment wherein I experience a high degree of certitude. Doubt is needed here so that my holy experience does not become out of tune with the mystery of life. Thus, doubt without faith and faith without doubt are static and inauthentic. The former is a refusal to acknowledge the mystery of life, and the latter is a refusal to accept the risk in living the mystery of life.

My experience of the human and holy Other is a rhythm of light and darkness, faith and doubt. When one is at a high point, the other recedes into the background, ready to manifest itself. Although I may experience a crisis when I am in the throes of doubt, my crisis can serve to promote my future faith. Although my ecstatic joy and enlightenment in faith are to be celebrated, my faith can also help me keep perspective when I am thrown into the darkness of doubt. I must doubt the Holy in order to believe, because my faith accepts that which I can question but cannot reason. I must also believe in order to doubt, because my faith makes available experiences that I can doubt and that consequently become more present to me. Thus, the human and holy Other draws closer and closer to me through the ongoing rhythm of faith and doubt.

TRANSCENDENCE

In my holy encounters, I am involved beyond my usual modes of interaction. I, as self, with all my free and limited humanity, intimately experience a union with, or being at home in, the mystery of reality. I am not coping with, exploiting, or controlling the Other, but I am in a mode of creative acceptance. I see the Other not in terms of conflict and problems, but in terms of harmony and mystery. This does not mean that I repress real difficulties in my life, but my transcendence enables me to see a more fundamental unity underlying my difficulties. For example, a person can experience many pressures in his work and his homelife, but his transcendence in love enables him to experience a deeper reality that helps him to accept and to cope with the many demands of his life. This "going beyond" the situation is actually going deeper into the situation through a different stand toward reality. My holy transcendence is to a different world, but not from the world, for in transcendence I am able to see the sacred-profane unity of life.

Thus, my transcendence is not some kind of supernatural or nonhuman activity, but it is a decidedly human experience. I find that transcendence is not a nebulous dream. It is a concrete and crucial experience. My transcendent experience, however, can be considered abnormal in that most people do not actively promote transcendence in their lives, but try to live only on the ego and body levels, opting for transcendence primarily in times of convenience or need. Too few persons live a life where transcendence is integrated in their total personalities and is a main motivating force in their lives. Thus, although transcendent holy experiences are especially human, they are also frequently outside the norms of contemporary life.

In transcendence, I also have the experience of going beyond my limits. I clearly realize that my limits are still present, but my perspective enables me to see their relatedness with the whole. I can take a respectful distance from them, thereby giving me a certain freedom from them. My affirmation, acceptance, and deeper insight into my limits prevent me from being seduced and shackled by them.

Furthermore, my transcendence in love incorporates a power that is decidedly beyond the willpower of the ego or the strength of the body. The peculiar power of my self transcendence is not concerned primarily with control or expression, but is oriented around a simple presence with, and for, the human and holy Other. In transcendence I experience a strength that is rooted in the core of my being and a confidence that allows me to confront reality more openly. This new ability to respond gives me a solidarity and rootedness, and my positive distance from the trivia of reality enables me to look more clearly at what is happening. Being-with-reality and transcending limits give me power that is rooted primarily in my option to promote the Other as my ultimate concern. My humble obedience to the most powerful force—the human and holy Other—gives me lasting strength.

SACREDNESS

My holy experience can be considered sacred in that the human and holy Other is my ultimate concern. We emphasize the word "ultimate" because all my experiences more or less include concern, but there is only one ultimate concern. In one sense, the ultimate refers to the value that is highest in my hierarchy of values. Every person operates according to a hierarchy of values and each person has an ultimate value—that standard, activity, or object which he values most. Sacredness describes what I most revere, respect, love, worship, and base my life on. This value functions as the greatest influence in my life. It is sacred. Of course, a person's highest value should be in harmony with the ultimate concern of his being—the human and holy Other. (In this context, sacredness points to the "object-pole" of my holy experience as being somewhat more than human, and of evincing such experiences as unity, transcendence, and love.)

The authentic lover always participates explicitly or implicitly in the sacredness of the Other. Although we contend that only the Holy is sacred, I and other persons can be made sacred in love. Thus, authentic love of another human being is a sacred experience because both of the participants come to experience the holy ground of their love. Their love for each other incorporates the Holy and makes them more available to the Holy, and although the beloved is not the Holy, she can become holier in and through love. I come to realize that since every person is oriented toward the Holy, love for my fellowman is always a sacred experience.

Ideally, if the center of my life is love of the Other, all my activities—body, ego, and self—will be colored by my holy disposition. This does not mean, however, that I love explicitly in all situations. I still maintain my sphere of interest—work, study, art, play, etc.— although it is implicitly influenced by my concern for the Other. This is not unusual because a person's experiences are always influenced by his main motivation in life, no matter what this motivation may be. If a person's life is centered around work accomplishments, all the facets of his life will be more or less influenced by his central motivation. The same dynamic applies to the holy person, and in this sense all a person's behavior is made holy.

We point out that sacredness is peculiar to the holy experience. An authentic man experiences only the Other as sacred. Thus, the quality of sacredness is important because it differentiates the holy self experience from other self experiences more than any other factor. Sacredness makes the experience of transcendence holy.

CHARISMATIC RELATIONSHIP

One way that we can consider the holy experience to be charismatic is in terms of its being an interpersonal relationship. My experience of the Holy—with other men or in solitude—incorporates a personal transaction between me and the Holy. This interpersonal dimension means that I, primarily as self, am involved with another—the Holy—so that I appeal to the Holy or respond to the appeal of the Holy. My interpersonal experience does not mean that the Holy is necessarily a Person, although this may be one of several interpretations of the Holy. However, I as a person experience the Holy, and in this sense the total interpersonal relationship can be called charismatic.

I also experience charisma insofar as I experience a holy presence that draws and appeals to me. Although this holy presence is primarily prereflective and numinous, I still experience it intensely. The holy charisma inspires me to transcend myself and to project myself into the Holy. The Holy breathes in a presence that affects me, and although this may sound spiritualistic, it is quite understandable because love does have this effect. The Holy not only appeals to me, but it also responds to my appeal. When I make myself available to the Holy, the Holy may respond in terms of sacred and charismatic love. This love penetrates me with a creative force that induces me to be more whole and holy.

My experience of the Holy can also be considered charismatic in relation to its charismatic effects on me. I gain a charisma in experiencing a creative power that promotes my own personality and inspires others. My power is not the power of ego control, but is the power of self creativity. I become more myself and am able to cut through the roles and facades of normal living to the core of my existence. Through my holy experiences I feel more grounded and at home in the world, and my presence is experienced spontaneously by others. Furthermore, my holy sight into the Other appeals to and encourages others to be more themselves. This holy charisma which occurs in and through love leads us to our next dimension—the way to the Holy.

LOVE

Love is the most direct and intimate way to the Holy for contemporary Western man. In love I open and give myself to the Holy, and I am ready to respond with concern and care for the sake of the Holy. The Holy also loves me in terms of its sacred charisma. The Holy is open to, available to, and gives to me. My love-encounters with the Holy occur in three basic ways: in solitude, with another person, and in a group.

My encounter with the Holy in solitude occurs when no other person is explicitly present. I am by myself in my availability to the Holy. I may purposely withdraw from my everyday world to be alone. I may be in the woods, by the sea, in a church, in any room, or doing nothing when I have a holy encounter. In solitude I am in a mode of simplicity. There are few distractions to divert my holy encounter, and my peace and quiet enable me to make myself totally available for the Holy. I do not have to be concerned about other things because my solitude frees me from things in order to be free for the Holy.

Although I am alone with the Holy, other people are present implicitly. My love of the Holy in solitude is also a love of my fellowman, because my love in solitude of the holy Other is in implicit affirmation of the human Other. For example, a person who encounters the Holy in solitude does not directly express his love to his friend, for his friend is not directly, but implicitly, present. On the other hand, when this person directly expresses his love to his friend, the Holy is implicit in his love. Thus, when one—the human or the holy Other—is explicitly loved, the other is implicitly loved.

I can also love the Holy when I love another person. Here, I explicitly express my love for another person, and in this human love-encounter I affirm and love the ground of our beings—the Holy. In my mysterious and transcendent love dialogue, I experience a charismatic reality that promotes a serene unity within and between us and that generates a holy ground which is greater than, yet the basis of, our lives. However, my love of man and of the Holy are not synonymous, because I experience the Holy as different but not separate from man and because I can encounter the Holy directly in solitude. Yet my authentic love for my fellowman always includes the Holy, so that love is, at least implicitly, a holy act.

I can also experience the Holy simultaneously and explicitly with another human wherein my love is focused both on another person and on the Holy. For instance, a wife's love may incorporate both her husband and the Holy in the foreground of her experience. Here the wife's love for her beloved and for the Holy are merged, so that the Holy is articulated in the presence of her husband. Although it is quite possible for a person, particularly a woman, to love both man and Holy directly, it is more usual to experience one in the foreground (explicitly) and the other in the background (implicitly).

I can also encounter the Holy in the presence of a group, such as in a liturgical service or in a celebration. My ideal is that people congregate and form a union with each other, and as a loving solidarity we present ourselves to and for the Holy. However, I must remember that although certain liturgical services can promote an encounter with the Holy, it is through love, not through a series of ritualistic acts, that I encounter the Holy.

If I exclude one of these avenues to love the Holy, the other will suffer. If I do not promote my love in solitude, my love of other persons will lose its holiness and therefore its wholeness. In this situation my love of others may progressively regress into a hysterical dependency or a histrionic control. On the other hand, if I try to love the Holy only in solitude, my love will also regress, often into a pietistic narcissism or into a schizoid existence. Our point is that since man is coexistence toward other men and toward the Holy, man and the Holy are inseparable in an experience of love. My freedom rests on which object-pole—the human or holy Other—I opt to accent.

Furthermore, my love of the Holy is dependent on my own and on my culture's state of development. For example, a primitive person's love of the Holy was probably highly influenced by his dependent and undifferentiated involvement with nature, and in this sense it may have been similar to the child's experience. Thus, the God of primitive man was probably embedded in the body processes and in nature. Likewise, contemporary man's dialogue with the Holy is highly influenced by his personal degree of maturity and by his ego-centered culture.

People often ask what is the humanist's relation to the Holy. We can say that the humanist, a person who leads a life of authentic love but who does not promote the usual notions of God and religion, experiences the Holy implicitly because his openness to and care for other humans in love necessarily incorporates the holy Other. Often, however, a humanist will eventually be forced to take a stand toward the holy presence in love. He will come to affirm or reject the holy Other in his love. Nevertheless, the humanist may not come to this confrontation for a long time or even for a lifetime. Even though his life is not explicitly religious, he does in fact lead a religious or holy life.

People also ask what is the difference between the holy experience and other self experiences. We have seen that my holy experiences are self experiences of love. However, I also have other self experiences that do not necessarily incorporate the Holy yet are closely related to my holy experiences. For example, I can have a self experience of philosophical wonder wherein I have a feeling of seeing in the light of the whole and of being whole myself. I experience a mysterious and transcendent unity with reality, and my experience may promote openness, growth, and fulfillment. However, since my involvement is in being and not in the Holy, sacred charismatic love is really not an issue in my experience. Likewise, my self experience of nature involves beauty, ecstasy, transcendence, paradox, mystery, etc. Again, although I am open to reality and feel whole and fulfilled, I am not necessarily holy because sacred love, worship, and charisma are not part of my aesthetic experience. However, such self experiences of being and beauty can lead me to or serve as springboards to the Holy, because in being self functions they lend themselves in the promotion of my holy experiences. Although they can stand on their own in a valid and necessary way, my experience of being and beauty may also transfer into a holy experience. At this point, my experiences are no longer philosophical or aesthetic but have changed into a holy encounter.

Finally, I may experience being and beauty in terms of or directly with the Holy. For example, I may experience being and beauty in the foreground of my experience, but my implicit presence to the Holy gives my philosophical or aesthetic a somewhat different flavor. Beauty, for instance, becomes holy to me insofar as the foreground of my aesthetic experience is permeated with the background of my holy experience. I may also experience being or beauty simultaneously with the Holy. For instance, I may experience the mystery of being and at the same time experience the Holy, so that both being and the Holy are in the foreground of my experience.

In the light of our analysis of love, we can consider prayer to be man's dialogue of love with the Holy. Prayer involves a response to the call of the Holy wherein the Holy invites me to listen to and accept the love appeal. Prayer also incorporates my call to the Holy to be in communication with me.

The language of prayer is not merely verbal. It also has other modes of expression. Prayer is basically a being-with the Holy, and without this presence to and for the Holy, words are meaningless. Words might serve to hide the Holy. The kind of language—verbal and nonverbal—depends much upon the situation. Our point is to avoid becoming fixated in one mode of expression but to promote an availability to all possible forms of communication. Contemporary man knows the fruit of prayer-with-others; he sees that his whole life can be a prayer if ultimately oriented to the Holy. The danger, however, is to become so busy that the Holy encountered in solitude is lost. Such a person's compulsion to be involved may exclude the involvement of solitude.

Our final point in this section is that I can be present to the Holy in other ways besides love. Although love is my most direct and intimate way to the Holy, my everyday life can be lived in the context of the Holy, so that all my behavior is in some way congruent with and linked with love—my fundamental motivation in life. I can also contact the Holy intellectually wherein I, as ego, reflect of my immediate experiences. For example, although theology is primarily a reflective and indirect presence to the Holy, it is nevertheless a way of grasping the Holy. However, if the theologian's reflective knowledge about the Holy is not rooted in prereflective experience, his intellectual contact will be lifeless, meaningless, and useless. On the other hand, since an ego approach such as theology helps to make the Holy more accessible and communicable, it can serve to promote man's immediate experience of the Holy.

UNITY

We have found that man experiences a sacred transcendent reality which he calls the Holy, and that his experience happens most intimately in and through love. In love, man also experiences a certain unity with the Other, within himself, and with the the world.

I experience a deep and intimate unity with the human and holy Other. I feel close to, in harmony with, and one with the Other. In this holy communion I lose myself and yet I feel most uniquely myself. Indeed it is true that I find myself by giving myself to the Other. I discover that it is good and enjoyable to be in his holy presence.

I also experience unity within my being, for when

I encounter the Holy the various parts of myself seem to unify into a harmonious whole. I gain a sense of integrity—a wholeness permeated with holiness. I begin to feel congruent with my experience, and although I may be at odds with myself in my everyday life, I now feel familiar with myself. I find the courage to admit what and who I am.

Furthermore, I experience the harmony and unity of the prereflective lived world—the world that precedes the reflective and analytic approach of the ego. My world of the Holy is a world to be with, not a world to be against. Although I may experience tension, my tension is of joy, fascination, excitement, respect, and mystery. My healthy tension is a result of creative growth into the human and holy Other, not a result of unhealthy problems. I am inclined to be in harmony with my pain because I realize that my suffering is in service of life-emergence. Even though I tremble, I rejoice in my trembling.

My unity in the holy experience helps me to experience reality in its unity. I feel at home with life. I see the untouched whole—the integer—of reality and I experience myself as being part of this integer. I do not feel at odds with reality, but my total being is experienced as being one with the whole of reality. I gladly admit that I am a disciple who is called to celebrate and to dwell on the earth.

CONSEQUENT POSITIVE CHANGES

My holy experiences do not remain in a vacuum, but they promote a number of attitudinal and behaviorial changes in my life. All the changes that emerge directly or indirectly from my holy experiences are positive, for they are rooted in love—the wellspring of holiness and healthiness. Even crisis, confusion, and disintegration can be positive when they are part of a growth process.

My holy experiences influence all of my experiences. My self experiences are more inclined to take on a holy aspect, and my ego and body modes of behavior may become less impersonal and more influenced by my holy disposition. For example, my work begins to incorporate a transcendent and holy meaning, and my body mode of existence becomes more spontaneous, alive, and emergent. My holy experiences encourage me to embrace the world so that even my day-to-day living takes on a spirit of holiness.

The mark of a holy person is love for reality, including man and the Holy. The holy person is a man of love. His holy love orientation motivates him to be available to others and to promote their welfare. We will show in our discussion of "lovism" in Chapter 4 that a holy person's love is neither masochistic nor sadistic, but his love is an authentic concern for himself and the Other.

Since love is the highest value in my hierarchy of values, it centralizes and influences all my other values. All other activities are second in priority to love for and from the human and holy Other. Consequently, I realize the importance of taking time out for the Other to spend time with the Other. I am careful not to displace the Other with work or another activity so that I find myself so busy that life passes me by. Thus, I structure my life so that I can encounter the human and holy Other both in solitude and with others.

If I am a holy person, people tend to feel at home with me. They know that a loving person can be trusted and will listen. My love is offered in terms of an invitation, not in terms of a forceful demand, and I promote peace and understanding. Through my holy encounters I grow in the understanding of how the world can and should function. I am prone to see the potential of people rather than just their present facticity. I see not only what a person is but also what a person can be. Because of my love, I accept, affirm, and appreciate the other person in his uniqueness and I respect him as such. I do not intrude on the other person's privacy, but I take a respectful distance toward him. I give him room to be.

I also manifest and am a witness to all those qualities which are congruent with a love orientation: peace, wisdom, understanding, acceptance, respect, compassion, availability, affirmation, integrity, pride, humility, etc. Although I never fully realize these qualities, I strive for and realize them throughout life. My holy transcendence also enables me to see life in terms of unity and integration, not separation and disintegration. Thus, I am unlikely to be seduced by aspects of reality—parts that are identified with the whole, but as a holy person I am more inclined to keep myself in perspective, and a respect for reality comes spontaneously. Being in touch with my self and the Other, I tend to look for the deeper and longer-lasting values in others and I tend to see through the social masks to the inner self of others.

Because of my taking a distance from immature, unhealthy, and phony situations, I may seem distant at times. In fact, a holy person is distant from the seduction of everyday and work life because he is more apt to transcend these situations. On the other hand, a holy person is the most compassionate of people in that he enters into man's humanity. He has the ability to suffer with (and to celebrate with) his fellowman.

In being holy, I am also a witness to the Holy in my culture. My holy witness is basically accomplished in my day-to-day living, so that my very lifestyle reveals the Holy in my life. My life becomes a constant and spontaneous manifestation of the Holy. My witness is not accomplished fundamentally by formal education, but through a lived-presence that is experienced prereflectively by others. I realize that the Holy must manifest itself in the culture, that the sacred is decidedly profane, and that the Holy is for the culture. I take on a responsibility to and for the culture because I know that a culture that tends to live only for the present and that lacks a holy and transcendent perspective becomes a fragmented and shallow culture. When a culture denies the Holy, it is committing cultural suicide. Unfortunately, contemporary Western culture tends to repress or to dissociate the Holy from the current of life and tends to pressure people to displace the Holy in favor of a life centered around technology and possessions. Our paramount point is that people are needed more than ever to stand up for the Holy in our technocratic-

secularistic culture. Without holy people the culture
will dissipate into a narcissistic theism. The holy
person is the vanguard and guardian of the Holy.

Another consequence of my holy experiences is
that I manifest a certain directedness in life. I seem
to know where I am going. My life has meaning in
the presence of the human and holy Other; life
makes sense. I know that life without the Holy becomes meaningless, and this sense gives me a solidarity. A holy person is usually reliable and dependable because he has a bearing and a consistency in
his life. Along with holy directedness, I gain long-
ranged values. I have a good sense of history and
of the future, and my presence becomes a dialogue of the past and future. Through my self experience of the human and holy Other, my life
becomes one of commitment and lasting values.
Temporary satisfactions do not become the center
of my life, but my life does take on a sense of comprehensive universality. Because I am always beyond myself, my most basic and influential values
tend to go beyond themselves.

As a holy person I also become a good person, for
I try to promote the welfare of the Other for the
Other's sake. I am oriented toward promoting life-
emergence, and I know that the greatest way to
promote goodness is to love. However, my love is not
a fantasy love, because, depending upon my degree
of psychological health, I implement my love and
thereby change the world. Through my love I do
good to the world and consequently I live a morally
good life. My morality is not a submission to a sys-

tem of abstract rules, but the spirit of the rules does permeate my life. Although evil does not fit in my holy life, I admit that my potential for evil is always present.

Furthermore, I become a man of faith and hope. My most important values are accepted mainly in faith, and my holy motivation is rooted in faith. In faith I accept the mystery of my own existence, and in hope I wait in ready expectation for its emergence. Being hopeful, I realize that if certain conditions are set, life or people will more likely emerge. Since I live in faith and hope, I am not bound by the clear and distinct—by what can only be communicated objectively. I transcend the seduction of scientism. Life in faith and hope becomes less complicated and takes on an underlying simplicity. I promote a style of play and simplicity in my dialogue with life. Faith and hope in life is no longer a trite statement, but it becomes a lived axiom.

My faith, hope, and love lead to trust. I feel at home in the world. I have less of a need to defend myself because I trust that the holy life in love makes sense. My trust is not an unhealthy dependency wherein I petition the Other to do things that are my responsibility, but my trust emerges from an affirmation of the sense in the Other and of its future emergence. For instance, I can begin to accept and understand death as a painful but integral part of life that gives my existence a deeper meaning. Finally, my trust in the Other makes me less dependent on things outside my personal realm, for I invest my life in love rather than in a peripheral accumulation of possessions.

We have already said that a holy person is charismatic. My charisma means that I inspire others toward looking in different directions and that I evoke respect and listening in others. My charisma is an appeal to others in love to be themselves. My charisma, however, is never forced on others. Its import lies in the fact that it is a dynamic invitation. My sensitivity to others in love makes others more accepting of me and says to others that it is good and acceptable to be yourself. My fellowman feels that I want his good; he feels that I am on his side and that I am willing to be for him. Thus, a holy person says yes to the wholeness and holiness of self emergence.

My sincerity is not a maudlin view of the world, but it is simply an honestly proud and humble stand toward the world. I grow in honesty in relation to my holiness. I am proud in that I affirm the privilege and joy of leading a holy life, and I am humble in that I am grateful for the gift of the Other. My pride helps me to affirm reality, and my humility helps me to listen to reality and be less inclined to impose myself on others. My pride and humility help me to have the courage and respect needed for a healthy and holy existence.

In my holiness, I am always going beyond to new horizons and becoming dynamic in my life-style. This does not mean that I am explicitly dynamic in that I am outspoken or draw crowds, though many people do have the temperament or ability for this type of behavior. Even though I may be quiet, I am dynamic in that I am constantly emerging and experiencing reality. Living a spirited life, I tend to lack defensiveness and to promote a spontaneity that impresses people. My spontaneous and charismatic love enables people to say that I am a holy person.

Finally, in and through my love with the human and holy Other I discover fundamental meaning in my life. I find and live the ground of my being—love for and from the Other. I escape the normal and mad life of maintenance and meaninglessness and I refuse to fulfill myself fundamentally with anything but the Other. I discover that life in love makes sense. I live this principle of life: self actualization is the gift-of-self-for-the-Other.

CONCLUSIONS

Finally, let us focus on man's holy experience as an existential and experiential reality. We have proposed that man's relation to the Holy is an existential reality. Man finds himself structurally and dynamically related to the human and holy Other. A yes to the Holy is a yes to man, and a yes to man is a yes to the Holy. Thus, if a person opts to be open in love to the manifestation of the human and holy Other, he owns up to what he is—orientation to the Other.

An increasing tendency exists to analyze God as a projection of man. The main theme of this approach is that man creates a supernatural being to protect himself from his limited and precarious existence. Strict Freudian believers see God as an illusion that fulfills urgent wishes of mankind. They analyze man's need for protection against helplessness and weakness, proposing that man projects a divine father figure in order to gain security.

Many contemporaries consider the traditional conceptions of God in terms of its being a mythology or an anthropomorphic wish-projection. Proponents of this "projection approach" say that the creation of the Holy helped historical man to understand his ignorance and to control his helplessness. This group proposes that the Holy served as a useful symbol of man's striving for perfection or as a meaningful explanation of the cosmos. Because of the advent of scientific and evolutionary views, modern religion should be an open and scientific search for the questions and answers of man and the universe. The *tremendum* should be met not with mythological gods but with a scientific testing of hypotheses about the unknown.

All these people in some way affirm the reality of an experience called holy, sacred, or religious. They focus, however, on the etiology of religion and/or the religious experience. Basically, they maintain that the religious experience excludes a sacred reality outside man so that the Holy is totally a function of man or society.

These and other criticisms of the religious experience should not be dismissed, for they contain much truth. They are excellent descriptions of forms of inauthentic religion or of modes of man's displacement of the Holy. The fundamental error of this approach is that it fails to account for the factors and dynamics of self experiences in general and the constituents of sacredness, transcendence, charisma, love, and consequent positive changes in particular. For instance, these persons do not admit the interpersonal or dialectical dynamics in their analyses of the holy experience, nor do they differentiate the consequences of the authentic holy experiences from those of the inauthentic. Since projection theory only incorporates the constructs of body and ego or similar and related constructs, these theorists futilely try to explain self experiences in terms of the body (id, primary processes, etc.) and ego (secondary processes, social self, etc.). Consequently, reality is perverted in favor of theory instead of changing the theory to incorporate the experience. Truth, however, is discovered in experience, not in theory.

3

Man's Experience
of No-thingness

I AM CONVINCED that certain kinds of suffering
are not only common but also crucial and necessary
experiences for a healthy and holy life. In fact, a
paramount theme of this book is that the pain of self
encounter—"no-thingness"—is the prelude for en-
countering the human and holy Other. We will first
focus on the common signs, symptoms, dynamics,
and significance of all experiences of no-thingness
and will follow this general analysis with a concrete
discussion of the stages of no-thingness.

THE GENERAL EXPERIENCE OF NO-THINGNESS

We see that man never lives in a vacuum, but that
he is always involved in the world and with others.
Although I usually take reality for granted, or experience it more or less intimately at other times,
the meaning of my world and others changes. Instead of being in direct or indifferent relation to
them, my world and others become more present in
their absence. The "things" that are outside but re-

lated to me take second priority to me. Emphasis is
on me rather than on what is outside me. The experience of no-thingness occurs when the world and
others recede into the background of my world, leaving me with myself in the foreground. No-thingness
is the gift of self confrontation. I come face to face
with myself. The core of my existence is thrown into
focus, and I am called to take stock of myself.

In no-thingness I am lonely. I feel the presence of
the Other in his absence. To a certain degree, the
world becomes a stranger to me. Yet, I yearn for the
Other. I miss people and want to be with them. My
lonely experience is more or less intense in that I am
in a state of tension between a striving to be with
others and an inability to fulfill my desire. Consequently, I am frustrated. What I want I cannot get.
Since my inability to be with another person does
not depend on the physical presence of people but on
their psychological absence, I may be lonely in the
physical presence of others.

I may experience healthy loneliness in being sick
or when I am faced with the sickness or death of a
loved one. The demands of illness, for instance, promote a withdrawal from the Other and at the same
time a yearning for the Other. The paradoxical bind
is that it is difficult to be sick alone or with others
because sickness simultaneously calls out to the
Other for care, physical and psychological, and to be
left alone. Consequently, illness without care by the
Other or without privacy becomes an illness in itself.
This type of healthy loneliness is temporary at least
in its acute phases and is realistic in respect to its
cause.

The loneliness of no-thingness permeates my existence. My yearning for the Other is unsatisfied, for although the Other is familiar to me, I cannot get close to the Other. I may search futilely for the Other, but the Other remains beyond my reach. Even though I may be deeply in love, my beloved, in my acute phases of no-thingness, becomes more present in her absence. Although the Other may be physically present, he is not psychologically close to me while I am in the throes of no-thingness. My cry for the Other often goes unheard except by myself. My loneliness may envelope me to such a degree that I too may become inaccessible to the Other. It may be comforting to know that the Other is there-for-me, but he remains "there" because I do not really experience him as being-with-me.

However, because I can progressively grow in a deeper sensitivity for the Other through the stages of no-thingness, my pain prepares me for the joy of being with others. Ultimately, therefore, my lonely experience in no-thingness is oriented toward the Other. Through self confrontation I am made more available to the Other, and through yearning for the Other I learn to appreciate and care for the Other. Thus, the loneliness of no-thingness is healthy when it is oriented toward growth in love of myself and the Other.

Analogously, a man who is physically separated from his beloved misses and yearns for her, so that his absence can serve as an opportunity to rekindle and deepen his love. However, his yearning in no-thingness is even more basic than this separation, for it occurs within him regardless of his environmental situation. In a very real sense, a person's yearning for the Other in no-thingness keeps him honest and promotes growth by pressuring him to renew his love for the Other. He can see and care for the Other in a new and deeper way. Love—the highest order—emerges from the quasi chaos of no-thingness.

On the other hand, unhealthy loneliness is based on a yearning that is oriented primarily toward one's own satisfaction—not love for the Other. Although decidedly human, such a person unconsciously exploits the Other. He wants to use the Other to satisfy his needs. He is willing to give, but only in order to receive. His needs frequently center around dependency, estrangement, or existential frustration—that is, a lack of fundamental meaning in life. This person is usually afraid to expose and openly give himself to the Other, for he is compelled to see the Other in terms of selfish gratification. The Other is a symbolic breast from which he must suck for life. Since he is unable to give himself unconditionally, his loneliness yearning can never be satisfied and his interpersonal relations usually remain temporary or primarily matters of fantasy.

In contrast to loneliness, I can be alone wherein I am physically by myself. I have more control over my experiences of aloneness than over those of loneliness. I can will to be alone; I cannot will to be lonely. When I am alone I can be psychologically with people, that is, not lonely. Aloneness can also be thrust upon me against my will. Nevertheless, I can transcend my situation by being very much alone and yet not lonely. On the other hand, aloneness increases the possibility of being lonely by decreasing defenses against loneliness. The key factor in healthy or unhealthy aloneness is whether I can opt to be open to and for reality. Aloneness is unhealthy when I choose to be alone because I am afraid to face myself and the Other. Whereas, healthy aloneness is ultimately in service of life-emergence.

Solitude occurs when I choose to be alone for healthy reasons such as self exploration, meditation, recollection, study, enjoyment, thinking, listening, and just "being." One of the highest acts of solitude is to do no-thing. Here I can choose to be alone in order to discover and encounter myself in no-thingness. In my solitude there are fewer things to distract me from my no-thingness. Solitude is always healthy, because it means creative discovery and becoming. A healthy life demands that I periodically take time out to be alone in solitude—whether this be in things or in no-thing.

Finally, withdrawal can be healthy or unhealthy. Healthy withdrawal can be physical and is aloneness and possibly solitude. I can withdraw from others to be with myself in no-thingness. Withdrawal can also be psychological, as when I withdraw from a group interaction and people say that I am "out of it." Being out of it may be a form of healthy withdrawal in that it is sometimes necessary to protect myself from the demands of a situation. When I am being pressured unjustly by others I must withdraw in order to maintain my sanity. I must also take periodic and creative retreats from the world in order

to re-create, and one of the highest forms of retreat
is to withdraw into no-thingness. If I never withdraw to find myself, I will eventually lose myself.

Withdrawal is unhealthy usually when there is a
refusal to face the fear of being hurt by the Other.
A psychotic person, for example, often withdraws
because he is afraid of being destroyed or of being
hurt by another. The paradox is that the psychotic's
admirable attempt to save himself via withdrawal
results in a chronic case of self destruction. Normal
people also withdraw for unhealthy reasons when
they are afraid to face unpleasant and unacceptable
aspects of themselves or of others. This does not
mean that a person must expose himself to being
hurt, but he ought to admit what is going on, and
then, if necessary, withdraw in a healthy way. In
order to say yes or no in a healthy way I must first
admit what is going on, for only when I know what
is happening can I do something about it. The most
unhealthy form of withdrawal occurs when I withdraw from myself. Since I refuse to accept the gift
of no-thingness, I become out of touch with myself.
Being alienated, I cannot authentically communicate
with the Other, for my self withdrawal precludes encounter with the Other. Thus, unhealthy withdrawal
is fundamental negation in contrast to the basic affirmation of healthy withdrawal.

We can see that in no-thingness I am thrown back
on myself—my existence is "de-pressed." I am often
de-pressed because I feel that I may lose the ground
for my existence. I feel lost in my no-thingness. I
also lose the familiar sense of the things around me.

The Other is different, values change, and my past world is suddenly outdated. I am psychologically distant from the world of things and I am "pressed in" on myself. My once-familiar world is foreign, leaving me with no-thing to grasp.

Being de-pressed, I may also experience guilt and frustration. I may feel that I have not lived up to my past expectations, that I am unworthy for that world out there, or that I am to blame for the emptiness of my world. Guilt may impinge upon my life —a guilt which says that I am responsible for my painful lot. My existence, being turned in on itself, results in a basic frustration. The Other—for whom my existence is destined—is beyond my grasp. No-thing is closer to me than others. My striving to make sense out of things makes me frustrated, and realizing that no-thing makes the most sense may leave me immersed in frustration.

I also experience existential anxiety and dread in no-thingness. My anxiety is a painful experience resulting from a crucial change that seems to have no purpose. I feel the ground of my life being undermined and thrown into a bottomless pit. My anchorage found in things gives way, and I am left in the middle of no-thing. There is no-thing to cope with and seemingly nowhere to go. I also dread losing myself in no-thingness. I feel primordially uneasy, and the primitive feeling of being permanently lost makes me feel helpless in the face of my no-thingness. To be caught in the vortex of no-thingness is the thing I most dread. However, my dread calls me back to the roots of my existence. In dread

I question the ground of my existence and I wonder about the possibility of any behavior whatsoever.

These experiences are often painful but necessary and healthy for deeper growth into life, because loneliness, solitude, withdrawal, depression, emptiness, guilt, frustration, anxiety, and dread in no-thingness lead to self expression for life. Although I stand in anxiety on the precarious ground of no-thingness, my anxious pain in no-thingness prepares me to be with and for the Other. In no-thingness I discover transcendent meaning and the freedom to dwell in and to enjoy the world. Paradoxically, my suffering enables me to say yes to life.

Thus, the apparent non-sense and the experienced pain of no-thingness lead to sense and to a deeper celebration of life. The gift of no-thingness means that I have the opportunity to face and own up to myself. For instance, I can learn to admit my limits. No longer do I live in the magical world of childhood where I can do and be anything I wish; fantasy will no longer satisfy the demands of reality. Now I painfully realize that every decision is a decided limitation, and I am forced to make decisions. It hurts to learn limits, but authentic realizations are possible only with an affirmation of limits.

Furthermore, living the experience of no-thingness promotes a healthy sensitivity. I learn to face and to be in touch with myself; and the more I am in tune with myself, the greater the probability that I can be in tune with others. I discover that when I learn to express myself to myself I will be more ready to express myself to others. My self expression becomes an art, much of which is acquired in the experience of no-thingness. My self articulation also becomes a wellspring of creativity, and new insights and modes of expression emerge in my loneliness. My new views are not just oriented toward the world of the arts, but more fundamentally my insights are new sights into my life. I find that becoming myself is the most important and fundamental form of creativity and that it serves as the ground for all other forms of creativity.

In no-thingness I realize that no one can give me freedom or make me healthy. I discover that I must earn my authenticity by learning and living the meaning of authentic dependency, independency, and interdependency. I admit that these projects are my responsibility and that although others influence and help me, no one except me can live my life.

The crisis in no-thingness also leads me to a re-evaluation of my standards. I now ask the questions: What is truth for me? How can I live my standards? How can I modify my standards so that they are in harmony with my experience? How can I make values mine without rejecting the past and those who gave me my values? This crisis is a crisis of my life—my identity in life. The fundamental questions emerge: Who am I? What am I? Where am I going? Whence do I come? Why should I live? What do I want my heritage to be? What is my life project?

I am also presented with the opportunity to admit what I am, so that I can come to a painfully exciting and new stand toward myself. I may discover that I am hateful toward my loved ones, that I consider myself inadequate, that I have little respect for myself, that I see myself as one with little value, and that I am unworthy of love and therefore unworthy of loving. In the same experience I may uncover the true love I have for myself and for others, the possibilities and talents that I never realized, true respect toward myself, and myself as a person of value and uniqueness, a person who is worthy of love and of loving.

Furthermore, my experience of no-thingness often offers me the possibility to change my life orientations. I may see in new ways or affirm past options in a new light. Being thrust into a crisis of self identity, I may discover new commitment in life or may reaffirm past commitment. New self discoveries, experiences, insights, possibilities, and limits are confronted. In certain instances I may even come close to despair, but from these depths I may rise to a greater level of personal integration. For example, a student may have to take a retreat from his life situation in order to find himself for a creative return. Depending upon his personal history, a person may even experience a psychotic disintegration that could lead to a creative reintegration. It is not rare to find a person become healthier from a psychotic experience when he accepts, integrates, and learns from his psychotic experience instead of trying to forget and to return to his previous state of mad maintenance.

After I have lived through my no-thingness, I also

have the opportunity to experience the Holy. Although my holy experience presupposes and depends on my experience of no-thingness, it is not a guarantee of an overt holy experience, but is only a preparation for the Holy. If I live through and own up to myself in no-thingness and if I remain available to the Holy, I will probably experience the Holy. However, my holy encounters may remain implicit for decades or for a lifetime even though my love of other people is explicit.

In short, the crisis of no-thingness is important because a person experiences a self confrontation that is a necessary prelude for the self experience of the Other. When a person discovers himself in the crisis of no-thingness, he becomes ready to present himself to the human and holy Other. His no-thingness leads him to being with reality. He is freed to experience love of the Other, wonder in being, and aesthetic joy in beauty.

Now, let us make some general observations about the dynamics and development of no-thingness. We emphasize that the experience of no-thingness and the experience of things are dialectically related. The more I find and become myself in no-thingness, the more available I am to and for reality. On the other hand, my experiences of things, especially other persons, have a great influence on my experience of no-thingness; my experiences of the Other —before, during, and after my experiences of no-thingness—will partially determine how open I am to my no-thingness. For instance, if people around me give me concerned support in my no-thingness,

my chances of living my no-thingness are much
greater than if I were made to feel guilty about or
encouraged to repress my no-thingness. Thus, my
self encounters with things presuppose my self experiences in no-thingness, and my experiences of no-
thingness presuppose my self encounters with things.

Although I constantly live in the shadow of no-
thingness, it may be brought to the foreground in
several ways. A direct experience of no-thingness
can occur at any time, but the most common and
fundamental way is to experience it at certain stages
in life. All the stages of no-thingness are basically
the same, although they also differ accidentally but
importantly according to the particular stage of development. These developmental crises are very important because they tend to keep me honest. I am
confronted with myself in no-thingness, and my decision to accept or reject the experience will determine my future growth. The fruitfulness of my
experience depends partially on my preceding life
history and experiences of no-thingness, along with
such factors as my immediate environment, culture,
interpersonal relationships, and values.

Furthermore, certain situations may evoke the implicit presence of no-thingness to become explicit or
they may rekindle a repressed experience of no-
thingness. For instance, a national catastrophe, a
personal crisis, or psychotherapy may promote a
self confrontation in no-thingness that is outside
or in addition to the developmental crisis. It is also
possible for a disciplined person to opt for some degree of no-thingness. Although this person does not
willfully control his no-thingness, he can opt to pro-

mote and to be available to a self confrontation in no-thingness.

From a theoretical perspective, we can see that the word "thing" has a special meaning in describing the experience of no-thingness. When used in everyday parlance, this word usually refers to an inanimate object; but when it is used in reference to no-thingness, "thing" refers to that which is outside but related to me. Things take on a vital meaning by referring to the worlds of culture, inanimate and animate objects, nature, people, and the Holy. Metaphorically, things refer to those situations and activities which are primarily "outside my skin." In no-thingness I am concerned with those experiences happening "within my skin" and primarily with those related or oriented to my self.

We can also discern that in my experience of no-thingness my body and ego modes of existence also recede into the background, and (with the exception of the negative stage) I am left with no-thing except my self. I become existentially introspective and spontaneously look within myself especially in my more acute moments. My body and ego, however, do not cease their functioning, for I am still very much in the world in these modes of existence. Although the accent is on my self, no-thingness involves my whole being, so that my body and ego are introspected basically in the light of the self. For instance, I may "look at" my intelligence or body in terms of its limitations, possibilities, uniqueness, or value. Our crucial point is that the "self" takes on the most significance and attention because the experience calls attention to the self.

Since no-thingness is primarily, although not exclusively, an experience of the self, the experience is beyond rational thought and decision; no-thingness does not lend itself to lineal and discursive approaches. In a certain sense I go out of my ego mind in the experience of no-thingness. Being a self experience, the experience of no-thingness is in the realms of mystery and paradox. Although my body feels intensely the no-thingness and my ego reflects on it, the accent is on my self—the most intimate expression of my being.

In the following sections I propose that man goes through certain stages of holiness and that ideally they are correlated with his stages of no-thingness. I relate each degree of holiness to a stage of no-thingness. Although most people experience the crisis within or near the age range, the ranges are not absolute.

NO-THINGNESS IN EARLY ADOLESCENCE

The initial encounter with no-thingness is a negative experience of no-thingness, which usually occurs in early adolescence, somewhere in the age range of thirteen to sixteen. The experience does not coincide exactly with pre-puberty and puberty, although its onset may emerge during or at the end of puberty. Girls often experience it a little sooner than boys. The "Catcher in the Rye," Holden Caulfield, or the notorious sophomore in high school are examples of people in this negative stage of no-thingness.

Although the young adolescent is not constantly and directly experiencing his no-thingness, he does have times of direct confrontation. Here he is bored; he has no-thing to do or be, and although he has boundless energy, he is tired. His behavior seems to be aimless and nonintegrated. It is. No-things appeal to him. He is sick and tired of life, even though he has scarcely lived it. No one understands. He feels alone. No-body and no-thing make sense to him. His world is a cosmos of non-sense.

Although the young adolescent periodically experiences the acute phases of his no-thingness, an orientation of no-thingness usually permeates his behavior. Like Holden Caulfield, he suspects almost everyone—"the whole damn world is phony." He sharply sees the imperfections and mistakes of his elders—especially those in authority, such as his parents and teachers—and he criticizes them with ruthless discernment, often to his elders' embarrassment. Parents are often at their wits' end to know what to do with this new edition of son or daughter. The object-poles of the ego and the body, such as work, science, structure, and feelings, recede into the background and make little sense. He takes keen delight in criticizing or breaking the rules; obedience is an ambivalent burden. Structure is a painful reminder of his no-thingness. He wants no part of it.

The distinguishing feature of this stage is that the person is left explicitly with no-thingness—not even his self. However, this person experiences his self in its absence; he feels a lack of his self. Thus, his experience becomes a decidedly negative experience insofar as it is not a mature self confrontation, for his self has not yet overtly emerged.

This experience is not absolutely negative, however, because it involves a new stand toward his own being, others, and the world, and it also leads to the first direct experience of self. Later, several months or years, perhaps this person will emerge as a self, and for the first time in his life he will have a direct self experience.

Out of his experience of negative no-thingness, the adolescent emerges as a self presence to reality. For the first time, this person directly actualizes and expresses his self. Again, the adolescent appears to change suddenly, and his parents' patience—for time to cure—has paid. No longer is the teen-ager bored or living in non-sense. Just the opposite, he is enchanted and romantically in love with everything. Suddenly he experiences the world in an entirely new way. For the first time in his life, he may begin to write poetry or to see life from a philosophical perspective. He still criticizes, although not from a sense of boredom but from a sense of romantic idealism. Before, nothing was possible, now everything is possible. His pessimism changes to optimism. Although the realities of the concrete situation usually limit his idealism and his future is uncertain, his basic enthusiasm persists.

Realities take on an added dimension, for they are now stimuli for romanticism, poetry, or wonder. His teacher is no longer an object of criticism, but he may become now a source of inspiration. This teenager begins to think of life commitment, which is a new experience for him. "Where am I going?" becomes a lived question from within, not an irritating question asked by someone else from without.

This emergent adolescent experiences love in a new way, for love now incorporates responsibility, respect, and commitment. Love is no longer only for the moment. Love points to long-ranged plans. Although his love tends to be romantic and idealistic, it is also experienced in terms of life projects; the teen-ager begins to think in terms of life commitment in regard to love and vocation. Since the adolescent's love now incorporates the sacred, he experiences the Other more deeply. In fact, he begins to feel a kinship with mankind. Furthermore, he encounters the Holy in solitude, so that moments of loneliness begin to make sense to him. He may, in fact, begin to cultivate such situations.

An explicit experience of the human and holy Other also emerges from no-thingness. In the past the young adolescent enjoyed an implicit presence to the Holy. Now he is presented with the opportunity for more direct holy encounters. Although his holy experience is not of the same intensity and quality as the mature and holy adult's, his experience does incorporate all the constituents necessary for a holy experience. The adolescent begins to experience a numinous and paradoxical transcendence embedded in a sacred mystery. He also begins to experience a new sense of dependency and indebtedness; and love, faith, and doubt become very real issues. In short, his encounter with the Other offers new experiences that he must integrate. He is initiated into a life in the presence of the Holy, and the consequent positive changes from his holy experiences begin to emerge.

The adolescent also starts to personalize the rules of his life. He begins to see new possibilities in structures. Structures begin to become opportunities for transcendence and freedom, not shackles as in the recent past. His transcendence gives him the freedom to increase his field of possibilities; and although these possibilities are initially played with in fantasy, they are nevertheless real. Morality, for instance, has new meaning for the adolescent; he begins to respect and be genuinely concerned for the Other. His standards for goodness go beyond the here-and-now and include the future. However, at times he may reflect and try to make explicit sense out of the holy experiences. Sometimes an adolescent will "think" very much about his new experiences, not so much in terms of the Holy but in terms of responsibility, and this ultraconcern for responsibility may take the form of temporary scrupulosity. The adolescent, especially one with compulsive tendencies, may become obsessively concerned about the morality of his behavior. This moralistic behavior is usually temporary and can serve as a means of growth by leading him to a true meaning of morality.

Parents and teachers are especially frustrated by this developmental stage particularly in its negative phase. They too often try with good intentions to get rid of the negativity. They see this experience as a problem to be solved rather than a necessary experience to be understood and affirmed. It must be realized and accepted that the particular kind of negativity and ambiguity of this stage is painful but healthy. Nevertheless, the adolescent must live through this stage in order to develop. If the future is kept in perspective, his negativity will make more sense. However, if the parents try to force the adolescent to become a mature adult before his time, the adolescent will only suffer needlessly and risk unhealthy frustrations in development. Parents can help by understanding and accepting their child's experience and give him a realistic amount of freedom to grow. They can be available when their teenager may call on them, and above all they can give him the courage through love to accept and live his experience in a meaningful and fruitful way.

This experience of no-thingness is the easiest of all the stages to live through because there is less danger of rejection, distortion, fixation, and pathological decisions. The adolescent's resiliency and ignorance decrease the possibility of pathological coping mechanisms. Furthermore, there are no direct self experiences to make sense out of and to integrate such as in the later stages of no-thingness. The adolescent's youth is often a saving grace.

On the other hand, the young adolescent may undergo unhealthy experiences of no-thingness. Because of a pathological personality, a person may never reach the stage of development of no-thingness. Or, a person whose basic needs, such as hunger, sleep, security, and love, have been seriously unsatisfied may not be sufficiently mature to experience no-thingness. An adolescent may also become threatened by the experience and regress to an earlier level of development or become fixated in nothingness for a long period of time. An example of such a person is the individual who is in his third decade of life and is still aimlessly roaming the earth in a negative no-thingness. The fixation, however, will usually develop into a pathological existence if not resolved in a healthy way, for the life demands of this person cannot be adequately integrated.

The young adolescent finds himself out of no-thingness. Functions of his self begin to emerge, and he has his first overt self experiences. Although he is a neophyte, he does begin the life projects of mature love, responsibility, commitment, morality, freedom, etc., including the self experience of the human and holy Other.

No-thingness in Late Adolescence

Our next stage of no-thingness occurs after the first direct experience of the self, usually in the late teens and/or early twenties. The outstanding feature of this stage is that it offers the first positive experience of no-thingness. The dynamics once again involve the recessation of things, especially the object-poles of the body and ego; but this time a person has his first true crisis of self identity. The world and others are distant in favor of the most vivid reality—his self.

In college, many students experience no-thingness most acutely in their sophomore year. The experiences of teachers and students along with empirical studies have shown that the sophomore year is significantly different from other college years. The lonely, withdrawn, bored, and angry sophomore is notorious. The apparently alive freshman may seem to turn suddenly into a confused sophomore whose value system has changed radically.

The sophomore confuses not only himself but also others. He is nowhere, has difficulty thinking of anything, and cannot get close to anyone. Intrapersonal crisis is dominant, and coming close to or being in despair is not infrequent. The sophomore is in school, but more fundamentally in no-thingness. This sophomore moratorium is a necessary prelude to a mature life. As a student once said: "One must become disenchanted with life before she can become enchanted with life."

The adolescent's recent idealism is replaced by a sharp self criticism. His self values, which he played with, are now considered from a different perspective. He sees his and others' limits, and ideals seem unattainable. He recognizes his needs for meaning and love in life and wonders if they will ever be satisfied. Commitment becomes very clear, but commitment to what and how? He asks himself if he will ever become a mature adult. He is confused as to who he is, his future is threatening and foreign, and his past is a source of painful realizations.

His present situation becomes meaningless and empty; things outside himself can no longer fulfill him. He begins to look at himself differently and starts to reevaluate his standards, which he used to take for granted. What is truth for him becomes a very serious question. This person can no longer habitually follow a system of shoulds that comes from without, but he strives to live according to fundamental oughts that come from within. Some questions emerge: What are obedience, love, respect, maturity, responsibility, and freedom? The classical questions emerge: Who am I? Where am I going? Whence do I come? Why am I? The accepted rules of his past are permeated with "why." Everything is brought into question in his no-thingness.

Since this person discerns his inherited "shoulds," he usually becomes more or less angry at his past—especially with his parents. He sees the limits and imperfections of these shoulds and he realizes what he did not receive and perhaps should have received from his parents. A common danger is that this person becomes fixated in this stage and refuses to grow until he has received what he thinks he has the right to receive.

It may be frightening for this person to realize that freedom and autonomy must develop primarily from within oneself and are not acquired from external agents. Frequently, a person looks outside himself for the source of freedom, such as parents or the structure of a situation. Many persons in this stage initially go through the process of rebellion toward their superiors and especially their parents. They make their pleas in many forms. "You won't let me be free." "My parents don't bother me—I cut the ties." These and other similar approaches incorporate a dependency in that this late adolescent feels that only the Other (superior) can give him his freedom. "If only this were changed, if I could do this, then I would be free" is a common adolescent experience that must be resolved. In other words, if a person constantly criticizes or brags of his freedom from his parents, he is probably quite dependent on them. He must learn to admit his dependency to attain true freedom.

Sometimes a late adolescent may physically run away from home, deluding himself that he has run away from his parents. Little does he realize that his parents within him—biologically and psychologically—can never be severed, but can be faced, understood, and integrated into the totality of his personality. When a person personalizes the assets and deficits of his parents within himself, he can authentically transcend them.

Responsibility also becomes a paramount issue. The late adolescent wonders how he can find the ability to respond to life. He feels inadequate, but nevertheless he vigorously fights his lack. Left with himself, he realizes that true responsibility rests on him and this is quite different from his past life. It may frighten him to know that in terms of responsibility he may now have to become in some ways a parent to his parents. He must be able to accept and understand his parents in all their positive and negative humanity, and he can no longer see his parents as, or demand that they be, perfect and divine. Nor can he lead a basically dependent and wishful life and be a mature adult. He must give up the ways of his past, but his future ways are uncertain and not yet attainable. His world is distant, and he does not yet know his self which must live in and guide his future. He is left in a bind, but his bind is temporary.

A common symptom of this stage is doubt. The

person suddenly doubts most of his values and standards that he took for granted. Religion is usually a prime target of his critical evaluation so that probably for the first time he asks critical questions concerning his religious belief. When he realizes the imperfections and errors in his inherited religious system, he may feel that he has been duped into living a phony system. This person may feel embarrassed and give up all his religious practices and beliefs, so that suddenly the once religious person is no longer practicing what he recently valued. He may sometimes attack those who profess to live the religious life, behavior that is often an unconscious attempt to make sense out of his own religion. Not all late adolescents confront their religious belief with such intensity, but most, if not all, do seriously question it.

The dangers of unhealthy experiences and resolutions are far greater in this stage than in the preceding one. A common danger is that a person's loneliness may become unhealthy. If a person has had past experiences of rejection or hyperdependency, he may become fixated on the absence of the Other. He may feel that his life depends on the love of the Other, because his salvation from his no-thingness is completely out of his hands. He loses all autonomy and longs for the panacea of the Other's affection. The bind is that these people are usually afraid to give themselves fully, for the very experience that they feel will save them, they also feel could destroy them. Therefore, they tend to go from person to person—never giving completely and never letting go completely unless and until the Other becomes too threatening. The greatest danger is that this person will move from loneliness to despair. All hope in finding the Other to fulfill the no-thingness is lost. It is not rare, for example, for this person to play with the possibility of suicide.

This experience of no-thingness may be delayed or frustrated for various reasons. For instance, the experience may be delayed because of a life situation which makes it less probable for this crisis to occur. The soldier in combat, the starving person, the immature person, and the mentally ill are a few examples. Why is it difficult to live through the experience and benefit from it? Why does one refuse the gift of no-thingness often in the forms of escapism, displacement, repression, regression, and sublimation?

The experience is painful; to be alone, empty, lonely, and feeling one's limits, hurts. People in the Western culture are usually conditioned to refuse or at best to tolerate pain. Pain is senseless to Western man. Living according to this pleasure principle, he finds it difficult to accept the fact that one can be liberated through pain, to realize that the road to maturity is fraught with the uncomfortable.

Furthermore, seldom is a person really given support or permission to be alone, because lonely experiences threaten others who may never have faced their own no-thingness. Elders frequently try to divert the young person's attention from his no-thingness. Although they have sincere intentions, many parents and teachers try to save the young person

from his suffering. They try to seduce the late
adolescent into activity—study, read, go to a movie,
dance, or party, walk, talk, join the service, work,
etc.—do anything except no-thing.

Many persons become anxious about their no-
thingness, often because they try to escape from
their existential loneliness. For instance, a person
fights a losing battle when he tries to deny what he
is, a lonely person in no-thingness. He becomes at
odds with himself, never really being at home with
himself. He is constantly restless and restive. This
anxious and lonely existence will not be resolved
until the person can face himself in no-thingness,
and therefore have the possibilities to give and to
be with others.

Finally, the experience of no-thingness is contrary
to Western cultural values. An overly pragmatic society makes no room for no-thing—the ultimate sin
is to do no-thing. One feels guilty if he cannot justify what he is doing, for the culture measures
worth in terms of what he has produced, not what
he is. This pragmatic infrastructure of the culture
makes it more difficult to cope authentically with
the experience of no-thingness.

We contend that this person has the right to suffer because if his experience is thwarted, he cannot
mature. Irritating behavior, such as doubt and criticism, should be allowed and understood in support of
the future emergence of self and other. Opinions and
feelings need not be condoned in order to be accepted, for there is room for disagreement if it is
based on love and respect. This suffering is part of

development and should be allowed to evolve and work itself out. If accepted, the suffering will disappear in time, but if the pain is not accepted, the pain will linger and become worse. This person may suffer about his suffering. If his loneliness is not allowed to be, a person may also develop inauthentic guilt feelings that tend to exacerbate his natural doubt and cover his authentic guilt. Soon this person finds himself in a bind—the more he doubts, the more he is guilty and his guilt produces more doubt.

If a person is allowed to emerge and is given support in emerging out of his no-thingness, he will come to his second direct experience of self and attain young adulthood. This self experience also has its idealistic phase, but it differs from the previous stage in time and quality. This person first sees and experiences the world and himself in terms of ideals. The establishment of the elders is particularly under his fire of criticism, and he usually finds it difficult to accept the impersonal technology and inhuman policies and structures of society. He is likely to be seduced by fictions such as love in itself is a panacea for the world's problems. He tends to see the world exclusively in terms of self experiences and finds it difficult to understand and accept the nonself approach of society. The impersonality of the establishment irritates him, and he considers it an impediment to authentic growth and self actualization.

The young adult may experience most of the established forms of structure as serious and unjust impediments to his freedom, so that he rebels against and resists the imposed rules that are not of his own making. He often dupes himself into thinking that he can live without many of the traditional structures. Later, he will take a more realistic and responsible approach to changing the structures.

In this initial phase, enthusiasm and sacrifice are paramount. Often the young adult is willing to make great sacrifices to attain his goals and to risk himself in his adamant stands. He tends to join subculture groups wherein he gets support and wherein his ideals can be partially actualized. Social movements, fraternal organizations, religious and political activities, clubs, hippies, and yippies are a few examples. This ideal stage is basically true as far as it goes, but it errs in its one-sidedness. Nevertheless, it is a healthy phase which people may grow through in various degrees.

Although an exciting and painful time, this initial phase should not last very long. Soon the college protester, the street corner militant, the headstrong celibate, or the enthusiastic married couple settle down. However, if fixation occurs in this phase, the person will futilely try to live an adolescent idealism. Such a person does not grow up, because he demands that reality conform to his fictive idealism instead of implementing his ideals in and for reality.

A person's holy experience may also be influenced by this idealistic phase. He tries to live a holy life at the expense of subduing his body and ego modes of existence. Everything is seen as irrelevant as contrasted with love. He tries to live holy love constantly, and often those who are loving are accepted. Everything seems so drab except love. Instead of the Holy influencing his daily living, he tries to exclude the everyday in favor of being explicitly and constantly holy. Holy, love, encounter, respect, honesty, etc., are the only important words, but he does not realize that body and ego functions are also necessary and healthy in living a holy life. Since he tries to keep the Holy constantly in the foreground at the expense of other realities, he may become hypercritical of things and reject the phoniness and imperfections of the world in the cause of holiness.

A person in this stage may have intense holy experiences and he may begin to make sense out of them. His sense, however, remains initially and primarily within himself, wherein he wonders about his experiences and about how he is going to implement them in his life. He may at first try exaggerated ways, such as changing the world only through good intentions—without time and study. For instance, a person who feels that his love will cure mentally ill persons is naïve. Although love is the basis of therapeutic treatment, the implementation of love takes years of education. Nevertheless, his idealistic phase is healthy if it is a step in the process of further growth. Since it is usually necessary for a person to play with his newly discovered holy experiences before he is ready to socialize them in realistic ways, this person should be given time to prepare himself.

If the phases of no-thingness and idealism are lived through in a healthy way, a person will begin the process of integrating his self experiences and values within his own being and within the world.

He will form a hierarchy of values in which all three
levels of existence play an important part, but in
which his self is the most important. Although his
life will center primarily around being an authentic
person, the values of having will not be excluded.
He will struggle and succeed with the difficult life
project of being a whole person. His body and ego
will be inspired by his self, and he will grow in becoming a whole and holy person. His enthusiasm
(*en theos* = in God) will become more rooted in life.

Since this decade of the twenties calls for life
options, such as vocation, commitment, and work,
this person realizes that his decisions in his twenties will probably carry him throughout life. In his
no-thingness a person first feels the pressure to decide what he is going to be and do, and the question,
How am I going to implement the who that I am?
remains unanswered. Will I get married or remain
single? Most people are forced to answer the question within several years, and if they wait too long,
it may be too late. They are caught in a paradoxical
bind. The longer they wait to decide, the fewer the
possibilities but the higher the degree of preparation. The sooner they decide, the greater the possibilities but the lesser the degree of readiness. Thus,
a person who marries young is more likely to be di-
vorced, and the longer a person remains single, the
more difficult it is to get married. Or a person who
committed himself too early may become a consider-
ably different person, leaving him in conflict with
his past commitment. Unfortunately, most people
are not prepared to make vocational or committed

decisions, so that their decisions are too often a matter of magical wish fulfillment instead of mature commitment.

In short, the third decade of life is one of crucial introspection and reflection. Reality is thrust upon the young adult. He is confronted with questions that he is usually not prepared to meet. He has to decide what to do, who to be, where to go. He can no longer keep these questions within himself; now he must act on them. It is a time when a person finds himself and how he is going to embody himself in the world. This person tries to discover the where and how of his niche in the world—how he can be a whole person and leave his mark.

NO-THINGNESS IN ADULTHOOD

The third differentiated stage of no-thingness usually occurs around the age range of thirty to thirty-five. The adult in his thirties is usually very involved in life, and since he has been in his particular style of life for some years, it starts to become crystallized. His goal is for things to run smoothly without drastic change. Thus, the critical change of no-thingness becomes a crucial and painful experience for this person. Once again, he is thrown back on himself, and he again experiences loneliness, aloneness, depression, self-identity crisis, commitment crisis, etc. This time, however, his experience is different from what it was a decade ago. He experiences his self as a self that has been incarnated and has been a life project, not so much a self that seeks reevaluation and initial commitment. This person experiences himself as more of an adult who has given up the ways of a child and the discoveries of late adolescence. Now he has the opportunity to confront himself as a man.

A person in his thirties feels his limits for the first time. Death makes its presence really felt, for death was not really a lived issue in his past life. He may already be past the halfway mark in his life and therefore he may be closer to death than to birth. Although this person does not experience death nearly so intensely as in later life, death does become an issue. In fact, the presence of death makes his life vital. His being-toward-death makes him anxious for life and encourages him to seek deeper meaning in life.

The fantasy life of his teens and twenties has almost completely vanished, and he finds himself rooted in the world. No longer can he live the ideal romanticism of the teens, at least not in the same way, nor can he play with the unlimited possibilities of life commitment as he did in his twenties. Now he is faced with concrete responsibilities that demand attention. He must live out his commitments and convictions. His psychological time and space are also drastically limited. For instance, his life options opened up many possibilities but also precluded others, and his experiential time goes by more quickly.

Particularly, this man begins to experience the limits of his body. Usually his flesh is weaker than in his recent and youthful past. The old axiom, "The spirit is willing but the flesh is weak," takes on new meaning. Now a person experiences his *own* limits —not primarily those of the world. He has to make some embarrassing effort to do things that he once did automatically. Aches and pains appear; personal and financial responsibilities face him; his stability appears to limit his freedom. Social life is curtailed; life is too busy; there is a paucity of fun. These limits of life are experienced acutely and often temporarily out of proportion to his situation.

A woman tends to think more in terms of her personal fulfillment—how satisfied has she been. Although she begins to experience her body limits, she still has just reached the peak of her sexual life. She may begin to play with the possibility of a promiscuous affair, especially if her sexual life has been unsatisfactory. She feels that her ability to seduce a man and the affair may offer the added advantages of escaping from her no-thingness. Soon she will be older and less attractive; so if she is going to fulfill her sexual fantasy life, she had better do it now.

This is most likely the last time a person can change his life orientation. He has a stark realization that he is immersed in life and he wonders whether he has made the right decision. If he waits another decade, it is improbable, although not impossible, that he will be able to make a change. If another vocation appeals to him, he had better take the risk at this time. However, this person's life situation makes the crisis difficult. He has settled down and has figured out a way to meet his responsibilities and to make sense in his life. He has acquired some authority or power, and a change would mean an abdication of many of these positions. Change for some people is seen to be an intrusion that upsets a smooth-running life, but others openly face the intrusion of change as an opportunity for further growth. The experience of no-thingness, however, does not mean that a person will necessarily change his life commitment; fundamentally it is an opportunity to explore and be more himself.

Religion becomes a critical issue—in its absence or presence. Being thrown back on himself in nothingness, he may seriously question if there is a God. He painfully questions the ground of his existence: Is there a fundamental meaning in life? He critically questions the God of his past—doubt is prevalent, especially with spiritual matters. In his no-thingness, he searches for a transcendent meaning—an ultimate concern that can give some ultimate meaning to the life that he has chosen. He asks many questions and often gets no answers. He wonders whether there is such a reality as a God, and he may come to the conclusion that there is not. Yet, he realizes prereflectively that the options he makes for his ultimate concerns will have a critical influence on his future life.

Many people find it difficult to live with the apparent non-sense in no-thingness, and a consequent repression of the experience is too common. A person in his thirties is still young and energetic; he has enough ego strength to run away from his self. Furthermore, a person usually has little time to confront his no-thingness, and he tends to look at his experiences of no-thingness in the same terms as the other experiences of his life—he sees it as a problem. He does not realize that no-thing does not lend itself to problem solving, but that no-thingness must be creatively accepted and eventually made meaningful. No-thingness is an experience for which one must take time. Otherwise, he will find time to be more and more meaningless. He must realize that some things are expedient, but no-thingness is beyond expediency.

If a person lives through his no-thingness, he will come again to new and deeper meanings in the things—the Other and the world. For instance, a husband will see his wife in a new light; he will respect her more deeply. His wife, in turn, will also increase in her love for him. The single person will see new meaning in his vocation; things will light up—they will make deeper sense. A person's life will not be a reluctant going through the motions of living. There will be a reason for being. His growth into freedom will enable him to transcend the embeddedness of his situation, and he will come to an inner solidarity and centeredness that will give an authentic style to his life. He will come to be the author of his existence, so that people will listen to and follow him basically for what he is—not for the function he has.

The thirties and forties are the decades in which to live and implement commitment. If a true commitment is made, a person will have direction and sense, and his everyday and work activities will be

permeated by the radiance of his self. A person's
busy life will not be mere business, but his activity
will be influenced by a force that makes himself and
others whole. His self values of love, openness, commitment, responsibility, transcendence, and so forth
will be given a greater degree of reality through
deeper articulation and implementation.

A person in his thirties also comes to a deeper
experience of the Holy. In his crisis of no-thingness,
a person's doubts of his religion and of God are
critical yearnings for the Holy. And concurrently he
may feel depressed because he feels that he is losing
the ground of his existence. His no-thingness, however, is an acute indication of the need for holy
ground and a sign of his desperate search for ultimate meaning. The groundlessness of his no-thingness is a desire for a meaningful ground for existence. He experiences more pressure than in the
past to face his need for the holy sense, and his
development and involvement in the world give him
a greater need for holy transcendence.

A person's history is an important factor in how
he will face his crisis. If he has grown from his
previous experience, he is more likely to accept his
present no-thingness than if he previously rejected
himself. A person who escapes his no-thingness escapes from himself and the holy ground of his life;
he is left with a rootless and meaningless life. However, if a person opts for the Holy, the Holy becomes the core of his existence, so that everything
makes sense in the light of the human and the holy
Other. His holy sense does not exclude the world,

which was the way of his past idealism, but his holy sense incorporates the world. He knows that his body and ego functions are necessary for the expression and implementation of love, and he begins the life project of integrating his love within his total being.

He brings his holiness to the world, and his witness to the Holy is actualized realistically to and in the world. People begin to recognize that he is a holy person—a person who behaves within and transcends the system. In a very real sense he takes on a new way of living, one that is centrally motivated by the Holy. Others experience his respect and love, and consequently they know him as a good man. They do not experience his holy orientation as explosive or intrusive, but as serene and strong.

This young man progressively discovers deeper meaning in life—his life has purpose. Since the human and holy Other is the highest value in his hierarchy of values, all his values are highly influenced by his holy value. He takes the Holy to the world, and his behavior is a radiation of the Holy; his everyday living begins to make significant sense in the light of the Holy. His love orientation liberates him for his everyday and work behavior, for his groundedness enables him to concentrate fully on his work. He does not have to worry needlessly about things, for things make sense. He enjoys recreation. He can play with things. His holy solidarity and ground also enable him to enjoy sex. It is a way of giving and of being, not merely a means to satisfy himself. In short, his routine—work, play, and love—becomes a celebration of the human and holy Other.

Love is his most important mode of behavior. His holiness liberates him to give freely and unconditionally to everyone and particularly to his beloved. He does not dependently seek a return for his love because his holy ground supports him. Paradoxically, however, he usually receives love, for he makes no demands on the Other. He can afford to love the Other for the Other's sake, and his love appeal invites the Other to love him.

Finally, this holy person is not seduced by the immediacy of things or by the perfection of fantasy. Standing on solid ground, he sees more clearly. He may become a mystery to some people, but a mystery that appeals, not threatens. People wonder how he can maintain his harmony and perspective, for he does not seem to be caught in the madness of life. People see that life makes sense to him.

No-thingness in Middle Age

The fourth stage of no-thingness, which occurs usually between the ages of forty-five and fifty-five, is often the most intense and painful of all. There are various names for this life phase, such as the involutional period, the crisis of the limits, and the dark night of the soul—all of which refer to the same fundamental experience from a slightly different perspective.

This person has gone past the halfway point in life, so he is closer to death than to birth. The reality of death overwhelms him, and he is forced to take a stand toward his experience of the "not-yet death." Although dying is the strongest limit he faces, sensitivity to limits in general permeates his life. Limits and a sense of loss are the key factors in involutional no-thingness. The faces of death and age increase his experience of limits. Limits surround him so much that it is difficult for him to see possibilities because his perception of a limited present and past frustrates his vision of a future.

In his involutional no-thingness, everything about his life tends to be considered as a failure or at least inadequate. He constantly asks himself if his life has really mattered to anyone, especially to himself. He has raised a family, but how well? Or, when has he loved in his celibacy? He has possessions, but how much? He has worked hard, but for what? He may ask himself: Have I really reached my aspirations? Others have done so much better. What difference does and did my life make? Who really cares for me? Who knows me? Darkness closes in, and this person sees himself as a limitation—as a nothing. He feels that he really does not matter. He feels like a zero—like a no-thing.

He focuses on his limits; his transcendent aspects recede to the background in favor of its rootedness. His self values, often those of ethics, life goals, love, and actualization, are critically questioned. This person says to himself: Time is running out on me. If I am not on the right course, it may soon be too late to find it. I still have time to find myself, but how, where, when? Has my life been true and mean-

ingful, or has it been a meaningless charade? The
often trite question, What is the meaning of life?
becomes a critically vital question.

Questions concerning the Holy also emerge. Have
I worshiped a false god, for what is God? What impact does God really have for me? What is my ultimate concern? Have I followed and supported rules
that are out of tune with reality? Is the church doing honest and good work? What is my role in the
church? Do these realities make sense? Yes and no!
Even if I should give them up, what would I have
left? No-thing!

His introspective eye also looks critically at his
own body and ego. This person is usually sick and
tired of thinking. He has found that reason is a
valuable means, but for what? Ego processes make
little sense without self processes—his ego cannot
give him what he is searching for. This person is
fed up with being a rational animal. The limitations
of his body also demand recognition, for his body is
weaker, less resilient and resistant, and more flabby,
painful, and tired. Physical fitness becomes a task
that is seldom achieved. Furthermore, the physio-
logical changes of the climacteric are usually correlated with his no-thingness and serve to exacerbate
his basic feelings of being limited, worthless, and
inadequate. For instance, a new crisis of sexual identity often emerges: Am I still truly a man, for I do
feel different? Sexual urges are less frequent and
less vital, and youth is a constant reminder of age,
a fact that this person cannot change. His crisis is
especially acute if his previous identity crises were
not adequately resolved.

Existential depression is also a significant experience. This person more or less experiences the most fundamental loss—loss of meaning. Life seems to make more non-sense than sense; everyone and everything seem distant and not worth attaining. This person is left alone with his meaninglessness and he feels lonely. No one seems able to reach him, and he feels worthless to reach out to anyone, and even though others may offer to help him, he often feels that others have forsaken him. He may feel that he is not worthy to be loved or to give love. How can a person who lacks so much be loved? Life has come to an end. He also feels that he has lost a good portion of his life—a life that he can never relive or regain. His limits push in on him; he is depressed. In his most acute moments he feels immobile, melancholic, lethargic, guilty, inadequate, and restless. His mood baffles everyone, including himself.

People in his situation, frequently the family, can reinforce his depression, often because, although they usually have good intentions, they may try to divert his attention from his depression. They try to get him involved in all kinds of activities or back to his old self—anything except to live the reality that he experiences. Of course, if he runs away from his depression, he runs away from himself, for he is himself in his depression.

Furthermore, this person usually experiences guilt wherein he looks at his past life, and forgotten experiences reemerge and plague his conscience. Past actions come back to haunt him and he tends to identify with them. He may condemn himself for acts for which he had absolved himself in the past.

Or, he may feel that he is partially responsible for the world's sad condition and that he has done little to make it better. His ruminating retrospection takes him out of the present and promotes a depressive and guilty withdrawal.

Although the dynamics of no-thingness are basically the same for men and women, there are sexual differences that we cannot pursue in this or in the other stages of no-thingness. One important difference, however, is that a woman in no-thingness is usually more involved with intrapersonal issues. Her menopause forces her to take a new stand toward herself, not only physically but even more psychologically. A woman is more inclined than a man to ask questions oriented within her skin and particularly those centered in her self. A man also introspects but tends more to focus on his ego functions, so that his work achievements—past, present, and future—are more significant for him than for most women. Although far from being exclusive, his critical eyes are focused more on issues outside his skin.

If this person rejects his no-thingness, he will suffer senselessly. A frequent method of rejection is to get caught in the normal and mad mode of becoming depressed about being depressed. This implies that the person is at odds with himself because he cannot accept his experience, the eventual result being an increase in depression that makes little sense. Thus, this person's attempt to escape from his no-thingness results in entrapment. In the extreme but not uncommon case a person may become pathologically depressed, so that he becomes immobilized and falls into despair. However, a temporary destruction can be creative or regressive. For instance, a psychotic involutional depression can be fruitful if it leads to a higher degree of integration. Sometimes a person may emerge as a better and healthier person because he has lived and learned from his psychotic depression.

If a person openly accepts his experience and if he can get support from those around him, he will come to new insights, even in his no-thingness. He will see the world through depressed eyes that will promote sensitivity to and understanding of experiences, a certain kind of creativity, an appreciation of death and limitedness, and the ability to suffer meaningfully. This person will also grow in wisdom wherein he gains a comprehensive perspective; he sees things in the light of history and eternity. Things are not likely to seduce him. He is not induced to become too busy. He is open to all points of view and finds sense in them. He realizes that it is non-sense to play games and that phoniness only leads to self destruction. He comes to an equilibrium, a balanced life-style, and his life becomes a research project. He researches the past and projects himself into the future; this is his presence to reality. Thus, no-thingness will again lead to a higher degree of maturity and to a new appreciation of things.

His love continues to grow. He now finds new meaning in solitude and he seeks it, for he discovers that solitude offers things that other situations do not. He clearly sees the transcendent aspects of love.

For instance, he knows that he does not have to be physically with a person to love him. He is also willing to suffer for the Other's sake, as witnessed in his loving tolerance when people are ignorant of realities that he clearly sees.

Along with his love, his work takes on a deeper meaning. He incorporates his work into a comprehensive plan of life so that it becomes an important act among others. He is not seduced into identifying his life with his work. He sees more value in being than in the possessions acquired from work. Yet on the job he is more stable and free, a stability that increases his efficiency.

Furthermore, this person realizes that his life is moving toward death, and he does not see death as a distant event to avoid, but he accepts it as a present reality. He knows that death is not simply an isolated act which people sooner or later experience, but that death is always happening—that he is always in contact with death. This person feels and lives death's presence as long as he lives. He feels death in the experience of his limits, in no-thingness, in wonder, in depression, in anxiety, in dread. He admits that since life and death depend on each other for meaning, the one without the other becomes meaningless. Living the reality of coming to death gives this person a deeper appreciation of life.

He enjoys pleasure not just as a matter of sensuality but more as a celebration. Although his body is now quite limited, it takes on new finesse and transcendence. Since he is not so likely to be seduced by the immediacy of his body, it emerges into a transcendent vitality. Pleasurable events become opportunities for celebration—a way of going deeper into reality, not of escaping it.

This person becomes a gentle-man; he is mild and gracious. Even if he is culturally or personally deprived, he attains a certain grace and simplicity of spirit. His self vibrates more than ever. It makes its presence known. His self fills him with spirit—he is full of life and he enjoys living. His earth becomes a place to celebrate.

Although his suffering is probably greater than ever, this person accepts it more and often makes explicit sense of it. He realizes that pain is an essential part of life and that certain insights into reality are only revealed in pain. He knows that growth without pain is a fiction and that his pain gives him the opportunity for sensitivity, mature suffering, compassion, and love.

In helping people, this person draws from the wealth of his experience and keeps things in perspective. He realizes that a good guide walks with a person and uses motives of appeal. He does not force a person to accept realities that he personally sees as valid, but he invites others to see and enjoy the richness of life.

His dark night of the soul also leads him to a new and richer experience of the Holy. His holy experiences complement him and vibrate throughout his behavior. His holy orientation does not mean that he is explicitly and constantly focused on the Holy; in fact, as in his past life, he directly experiences the Holy only in special situations. On the other hand, however, his explicit experiences of the Holy do increase in frequency and quality, and his implicit presence to the Holy becomes more and more present in the foreground of his everyday behavior. Although he is involved in life with much more authority and responsibility and is more accountable and responsible than ever before, his behavior is permeated with love.

This person emerges from his depressive and guilty no-thingness to the ground of life—the Other. If he does not find or renew his ultimate concern of holiness, he will get caught in the death of depression or will try to escape from his no-thingness. The holy person in this involutional stage faces death and finds life, and his no-thingness is fulfilled by the human and holy Other.

No-thingness in Old Age

With the exception of death, the last critical stage of no-thingness occurs in the second half of the sixties, usually after retirement. The person's body is much weaker than in the past and is rapidly becoming weaker. Reflexes have slowed down; eating and sleeping have changed. Although physical activity can and should be maintained, the body cannot be actualized as much and as vigorously as before. This person as ego is no longer involved as he used to be, for usually he is no longer working professionally. Our paramount point is that the functions and values of the body and ego become less and less significant in contrast to the functions and values of the self. The self takes over more than ever, for this person is left in time primarily with his self.

Usually this person's situation changes radically. If a worker has retired, he must now learn, to a large degree, a new way of life. He may suddenly find that he has time on his hands and he does not know what to do. He no longer has to go to work. It is up to him to make his time meaningful. The housewife also has to make a new adjustment, for she is suddenly left with more time with her husband, and this has never happened before. Her situation has fundamentally changed by the very presence of her husband. If widowed, he (or more often she) finds himself alone. This person must find new friends or find old friends in a new way. No longer can he expect the companionship of his wife; no longer can he depend on his wife to take care of the house and of him. A single person may have no-thing even more acutely. A single person too often has to face his lonely no-thingness alone. Even if this person lives in a community, he finds that many of his friends have died or have left and he is in a different situation, such as a retirement home. Regardless of his particular situation, the old person must go out into the world anew.

Death is directly in front of this person; death is impossible to deny. Many friends and relatives may have already died, and youth are a constant reminder of his age. This person feels death more and more in his body, and task-oriented behavior of his ego makes less sense. Depression emerges to various degrees and for various reasons, for this person feels that he is losing himself. He may also experience a loss of self esteem in his loss of bodily and functional powers. His life is nearing its end, and he begins to reflect on it. Since he naturally sees life in perspective and realizes that he cannot live it over again, he is forced to accept what has happened. He no longer has the energy to run away from death—death has caught him.

Western culture makes it especially difficult for this person to accept his no-thingness. Since Western man is judged on his ability to produce, if he can no longer produce, he is seen as a burden—someone to get out of the mainstream of life. People in the Western culture seldom listen to older people. They are, at best, people to tolerate. Geriatric sections of hospitals and homes for the aged are often living testimonies to this perverted view of old age. Too often old people are put in geriatric hospitals, not because they need psychiatric or medical help, but because they interfere with the lives of younger people. Even old people are conditioned into thinking that they always get in the way and are not wanted. They reluctantly withdraw so that they do not interfere with the lives of their children. A paradox exists in that the children are ready to give to their parents materially in terms of bodily comfort and financial security, but not spiritually in terms of love, care, understanding, and appreciation. These self experiences are the very ones an old person needs, yet they are the ones that are withheld.

How the aged person accepts and lives through his no-thingness depends largely on his previous life and experiences of no-thingness. If a person has made healthy options toward his past critical experiences, this period of no-thingness can be relatively easy but nevertheless painful. For instance, if this person has already gone through the crisis of the limits successfully, he is likely to accept this stage. Here he dwells in his no-thingness and gains insight in himself and in life and death. He will come to a new level of wisdom and higher integration.

His life takes on its deepest meaning, and his love really becomes transcendent. He does not need the constant reassurance of sex to affirm his love, and he knows that he can still deeply love the dead, who live in his appreciation of death. He is glad to be left with a lot of time, for he enjoys this time to live. Life can no longer bother him—he is too close to death and life. His body and ego demands may bring pain, but not stress. He sees life in the light of death, and this lived insight makes his life take on a new vibrance. By accepting death, he becomes full of life.

On the other hand, a person who does not renew himself in no-thingness usually falls into a depressive stagnation. He becomes depressed about being depressed, tired of being tired, bored with being bored, sick of being sick, and weak about being weak. This person fights himself, and since he has little energy, he wastes away. Initially, this person will often try to find things to do to fill his time and no-thingness. But after a short time, he is left with himself in no-thingness; he has no-thing. Faced with no-thing and not knowing how to accept and face himself, he identifies with no-thing. Thus, he becomes restive and restless. Depression overwhelms him, and he disintegrates into no-thingness. Eventually, this person kills himself—physically or psychologically.

It is relatively rare to see a happy old person. It is especially sad because this is the time when a person can re-create and celebrate life, for he has the time and above all the knowledge and wisdom. Even if society does reject him by tolerating him, he can still transcend his situation. However, if a person has identified his life with his function in life, when he retires he retires from life and not just from his function in life. Consequently, it behooves an older person to prepare for his retiring years long before he is retired. A person does not adjust just because he wishes it. His preparation should be mainly internal—a solid evaluation of his values. For example, the values of having and doing mean less in retirement—being predominates. Also, interests like learning how to enjoy and celebrate everyday activities such as walking, eating, talking, and traveling can be crucially significant. Individual interests like reading, music, sports, and social activities can also help a person to enjoy time in a meaningful way.

We have mentioned that if a man has identified his life with his work, he will lose his life. On the other hand, psychological and cultural influences make work crucially important for most retired men. Most men are workers, and life without any work can be critical in itself. In this light, it is usually helpful for a man to find some part-time work within and/or outside his home. Our main point is that he learn to enjoy his work; to see it not as a burdensome task but as a pleasant and meaningful activity. Parenthetically, work is not so important for most women because of their different psychological and environmental situations.

If the Holy does not emerge in a person's sixties, death will probably occur prematurely. Death will manifest itself initially in the spiritual realm, then psychologically, and finally biologically. This person will be left without any saving meaning in life: ultimate concern will be present only in its absence. He will find it impossible to live without a ground for his being, so that the time he has will be time for no-thing. No longer can he escape from his yearning for the Holy. The Holy has caught up to him in time. This person can no longer use the weak functions of his body and ego as self escapes, for without a meaningful and ultimate ground his ego becomes useless and his body feels no sense in living.

Although a tragedy, this crisis can be prolonged into the seventies and longer. Because of certain situational factors, an old person may be suspended in a nebulous field of no-thingness. People, at home or away from home, may unconsciously help an old person to maintain himself in no-thingness, and although they prevent him from dying with minimal institutional care, they seldom take time to listen to or to talk with an old person. In helpless collusion, an old person may play the game of being old (sick, useless, and dependent) and slowly dissipate in his no-thingness.

If a person has repressed the Holy in his past, it becomes very difficult to admit the Holy; however, it is not impossible. This person must be willing to suffer in order to rekindle his repressed years of no-thingness before he is liberated to and for the Holy. He must be willing to pay the price of his self denial in terms of depression, guilt, and loneliness. On the other hand, a person who has lived through his no-thingness and has found the holy ground of his life will find it relatively easy to reach a climax of holi-ness. His explicit encounters with the Holy will be more and more explicitly permeated with the Holy. This old person's time is filled with meaning and he grows in time toward living in an overt state of holiness. This person will gladly accept his no-thing-ness and he will come to the deepest and richest ex-perience of love. His life will become a constant cele-bration of the human and holy Other.

Finally, a holy old person is beautiful. He may frighten people in that holiness and oldness are not congruent with a production-centered culture. Others may try to disregard him, but it takes effort to dis-miss him, even though he speaks little. His silent holiness speaks for itself. One of Western culture's greatest faults is that people seldom listen to the wisdom and holiness of healthy old people. These old people disclose the pathology of Western culture in witnessing to the wholeness and holiness that are lacking in the culture.

FINAL NO-THINGNESS

The final encounter with no-thingness comes in death. A dying person is faced with the meaninglessness of chaos and the meaningfulness of order. Whether or not the Holy fulfills a person's no-thingness depends on his life.

4

Man's Displacement
of the Holy

WE HAVE SEEN that if a person emerges from his no-thingness, he will come to a deeper and more meaningful experience of reality. He will find the ground of his being—love for and from the human and holy Other. However, what happens when a person does not accept his no-thingness and consequently the Other? Our concern in this chapter is to answer these questions by proposing that man replaces the Other with substitute objects primarily to fulfill and escape from his no-thingness. Although it is important to study man's displacement of his fellowman, our accent in this chapter is on man's displacement of the holy Other rather than the human Other. However, we emphasize that a displacement of the Holy eventually and necessarily leads to a displacement of man. Before presenting some common and concrete modes of displacement, we will begin with a more general and abstract picture of man's displacement of the Holy.

MAN'S DISPLACEMENT OF THE HOLY

Theoretically, the process of displacement refers to a distortion of the appropriate goal of a motive whereby a person replaces the true but inaccessible or threatening goal with a substitute object. A classic example is the workingman who for various reasons cannot directly express his anger toward his boss, who originally evoked the anger. Arriving home, he immediately becomes angry with his unsuspecting wife. In this case the wife acts as the substitute object that replaces the true but inaccessible goal of his anger—the boss. Energy that was originally directed toward a specific situation (toward his boss) is now invested or expressed in a substitute situation (toward his wife). Thus, instead of openly admitting to his anger toward his boss, the husband tends to repress what he would really like to do, and his "angry energy" is "let out" on his wife. Although he gets some relief from his displaced expression, he not only exploits his wife but he also prevents himself from owning up to and understanding his feelings toward his boss.

In a similar manner, a person can repress or distort his movement toward the human and holy Other by replacing the Other with a substitute object. In this case, a person's desire or "energy" is not directed toward its proper goal—the Holy—but is displaced in a substitute activity. It is emphasized that when a person displaces the Holy he tries to satisfy his desire and thereby gain a sense of fulfillment. In fact, his displacement of the Holy can and often does make sense. He escapes from his nothingness and gains a precarious and temporary fulfillment. The substitute activity does fulfill him, although it is an inadequate fulfillment. However, the contradiction remains. Such a person can never actualize himself, for he does not admit the proper object of his innate desire. In his attempt to become whole he displaces the Holy and becomes unwhole.

Another important point is that a displacement implicitly refers to the object that originally evoked the response. The husband, who inappropriately displaced his anger on his wife, betrayed the goal of his angry motive—his boss. In addition, he is encumbered with guilt and shame. If his wife were to wait for a while, she would be able to discover the real reason for her husband's annoyance, that is, the proper object of his anger—his boss. Likewise, the displacement of a person's holy desire implicitly refers to the Holy, since the displacement is an attempt to fulfill the need for the Holy.

Thus, a person's futile attempts to displace the Holy are indications of the Holy in its absence, and his methods of hiding the Holy betray his desire for the Holy. Our task is to discover and to rekindle the Holy hidden in the displaced activities. Otherwise, we contend that man will lose the Other and himself and consequently lead a meaningless existence.

We have seen that a yearning to be fulfilled exists initially and most acutely in the experience of nothingness. A person experiences a desire to be fulfilled—to be something, to be someone, to be him-

self. He wants to find existential meaning in life
and to achieve a sense of well-being and happiness.
Since only love can fulfill him, love for and from
the Holy and man, he must let the Holy reveal itself. However, the desire for the Holy is absent, repressed, rejected, or hidden in too many people. In
his attempt to make sense out of life a person might
displace the Holy, becoming neither whole nor holy.
If he rejects the Holy, certain consequences emerge.

Most fundamentally this person loses the ground
for his existence. He searches desperately for something to give him a valid orientation—a solid ground
in which to root his life. He constantly tries to discover something that will fulfill his no-thingness and
make him be himself. This person does not realize
that only the Other, including the Holy, can fulfill
him. Since he does not or cannot let the Holy save
him from his no-thingness, his search for meaning
leads to meaninglessness.

Although a person does reach a sense of meaningful wholeness in displacement activities, it is temporary and inadequate. This person develops into a
lived contradiction. His striving for ground leaves
him groundless. Since his efforts to be whole preclude the Holy, he is left fragmented, and his displacement of the Holy leads to a personal displacement. He cannot find his place in life, for he cannot
live the fact that his place is to love man and the
Holy. He fails to realize that he can be wholly himself only by giving himself to man and to the Holy.
Thus, his rejection of the holy Other leads to a rejection of himself and the human Other. Further-

more, a person's activity for replacing the Holy is
itself perverted and displaced because his activity
is made to satisfy a need (for the Holy) that is
outside its realm. For example, when sex is used
to satisfy the need for love, not only is the Other
displaced but the sexual act itself is exploited and
therefore perverted. Thus, a circular causality is
promoted. A person's attempts for fulfillment via
displacement become less and less fulfilling and simultaneously promote a greater need for meaningful fulfillment.

The displaced person constantly feels incomplete
and guilty. His incompleteness does not stem from
his dynamic restlessness, but from his fragmenta-
tion. He feels that an important part of his life is
missing, for he experiences the Holy in its absence,
and his sense of not being whole leads to guilt. Although he is usually not conscious of what he is
guilty about, guilt permeates his existence.

Other experiences also emerge from the rejection
of the Holy. A person becomes existentially frustrated, for his existence is basically blocked from
further self emergence. He also becomes chronically
depressed in that he has lost fundamental meaning
in life. His loss is not of this or that person, but is
more fundamentally a loss of the Other. Furthermore, his displacements ultimately serve to exacerbate his depression. The more this person displaces,
the more he becomes depressed.

This displaced person is also bored. His frantic
boring into life for meaning results in a subtle but
fundamental sense of tiredness. He becomes sick

and tired of searching, and because of a lack of meaning he becomes bored to death with life. Everything becomes boring. Things often become ends in themselves and lose their meaning without the Holy. A lack of ultimate concern makes life sterile and helpless, since there are few possibilities for lasting fulfillment. His boredom often leads to a lived despair wherein life makes no fundamental sense, and lived despair may lead to ultimate despair—death. Since there is not sense in living, death becomes the only solution to meaninglessness.

It might appear that the displaced person's experiences are the same as the experiences of a person in no-thingness. Indeed, there are similarities because both people are in no-thingness, though in different ways. The displaced person tries to escape from his no-thingness instead of living through it. In fact, he is chronically afraid of no-thingness, and his displacement of the Other is a futile and frantic attempt to escape from the vortex of no-thingness. Since he runs constantly and anxiously from his being lost in no-thingness, he loses everything. His experiences of loneliness, anxiety, depression, etc., do not promote discovery, growth, and meaningfulness; on the contrary, they are indicative of adequacy, maintenance, and meaninglessness. Since a displaced person does not openly admit that he is his experiences, his escape from "them" is also an escape from himself. On the other hand, a person who accepts his experiences in no-thingness finds himself and the Other.

If a person does find himself in this bind of mean-

inglessness, why does he refuse to accept his no-
thingness? It is meaningful for us to review some
of the reasons for escaping from no-thingness. We
saw that the experience of no-thingness is a painful
experience, and most people are conditioned to reject pain. They try to live according to a pleasure
principle, that is, a lack-of-pain principle. Western
man automatically tries to get rid of pain because
it is non-sense to him, and at best he merely tol-
erates it.

This person also finds himself alone, lonely, empty,
yearning, limited, depressed, lost, anxious, and no-
thing. All these experiences are not supported by
the culture or by most people. The cultural value
system of production and pleasure is incongruent
with these experiences. Seldom is a person given
permission to be, support in being, and affirmation
of being left alone in his no-thingness. Furthermore,
people are afraid of possible chaos in no-thingness
and therefore have a compulsive need to make order
of things. For these and for many individual reasons, it becomes difficult for a person to accept his
no-thingness.

There are several kinds of persons who have difficulty with no-thingness. An immature person does
not willfully reject his yearning for the Holy, because he has never really had the opportunity to
experience no-thingness. Although a child can be
mature for his age, he is too immature to encounter
the Holy directly. He is in a process of not-yetness
in regard to the Holy. Although his immaturity may
be due to an impoverished environment or he may

be fixated at an earlier stage of development, an immature adult has never really reached the level of development wherein he can confront the Holy as a mature adult. Nevertheless, he can come to a simple presence to the Holy. Although a mentally retarded person may not have much ego ability to support and promote his yearning in no-thingness, he too may come to a pure but undifferentiated holy experience.

On the other hand, a neurotic person may try to repress his desire for the Holy, and consequently he lives an anxious existence. Since he is unconsciously forced to use various defense mechanisms to repress his holy desire, he fights a losing battle. The more he represses, the stronger his desire becomes. He lives in a state of unawareness and of being out of touch with himself. The neurotic person differs from the person of bad faith, because this person willfully rejects the Holy and he consciously promotes displacement of the Holy for his own benefit. This person's no to the Holy is fundamentally willful, whereas the neurotic person's negation is basically unconscious. However, a neurotic person may not close himself to the Holy, although he does repress other important experiences. This person lives a neurotic yet holy life.

A psychotic person may experience the Holy in an undifferentiated, primitive way especially in the initial and acute phases of psychosis. Since psychosis is usually some kind of ego disintegration, it does not necessarily preclude the self processes, which may include a psychotic experience of the Holy. Since a psychotic person has little ego control, other experiences intermingle and infringe on his holy experience. His experience becomes increasingly confused, for the more chronic the psychosis, the more self-disintegration results. Thus, in time, this psychotic person, too, risks losing contact with the Holy.

If a psychotic person did have holy experiences before his illness, he may have more intense but more confusing experiences of the Holy in his psychotic mode of existence. In fact, a psychotic experience may be fruitful for a person in that he comes to a fuller appreciation of the Holy in and through his psychotic experience and in that his psychotic disintegration is in service of a future and a healthier reintegration. A person's rejection of the Holy may also result in a psychotic episode wherein he is forced to face himself and the Holy. However, not all psychotic persons experience the Holy, for a person may be too immature, regressed, disintegrated, or repressed to be capable of this experience.

The most common type of person who displaces the Holy is the normal person. Although this person is not mentally ill, he is not healthy. By satisfying his basic needs, he is able to maintain himself and prevent unhealthiness. He manages to adjust to reality by giving the minimum demanded by himself and the Other. On the other hand, this normal person does not actualize himself and the Other to the fullest possible degree, nor is the Holy his constant and consistent ultimate concern. Many normal people lead a marginal existence in that they maintain peripheral contact with the Holy by such activities as passively attending liturgical services, by routine prayer, and by appeal to the Holy in times of want. However, the Holy is not the main motivating force in their lives, but is more like a fringe benefit. Although the normal person does not willfully promote displacement of the Holy, he may find himself displacing the Holy because of such factors as personality needs, environmental stress, and cultural pressures. The paramount point is that he tries to escape from his no-thingness by replacing the Holy with substitute objects, resulting in a normal and meaningless life. His attempt to fulfill himself without the Holy is a normal form of madness. Some of these normal modes of madness—man's displacements of the Holy—are the subjects for our next analyses.

POWERISM

"Powerism" is a neologism that refers to a life-style of people who invest their desire for the Holy in power. These persons transform their will to the Holy into a will-to-power, and consequently they operate primarily according to the will-to-power. Power is a valid and necessary mode of functioning, but when power becomes the central motivating force, it becomes "powerism."

This man makes himself the center of the universe; he sees himself as the most important reality. Rather than orienting his life toward the Other, he demands that life center around him. Instead of becoming allocentric, he becomes egocentric. Since most of his time and energy is invested in his ego processes, his ultimate concern is his own ego. Ego values become his ultimate values; reflective thinking and choosing, adjustment, control, objectivity, organization, etc., are primary. Life is a business for this person, and he becomes an organization man.

The power man tries to be completely independent and to control everything. Since he operates almost exclusively on an ego level, he tends to be coldly efficient and superficial. He does not accept limits in himself or in others, because he wants to be perfect; in fact, he wants to be God. His approach is based on what *he* thinks should happen. He has only to push the proper button and things will happen. His body is controlled unless he decides to indulge in bodily pleasure, for bodies—his own and others'— are only means toward an end. He also represses his self, for faith, risk, mystery, paradox, etc., are too threatening and are beyond control. He cannot afford to admit them. Experiences that are ends in themselves are meaningless, for everything is conditional and a means toward something else. The end is himself. We can say that he tries to redeem himself from his no-thingness because he alone tries to make himself something.

Since this person deifies himself, he thinks he knows what is best for everyone. In his closed presence to the others he imposes his own frame of reference on others. His approach is in terms of either/or. He will never admit to paradox or ambiguity. Since he is not truly capable of considering the other person's viewpoint, it is impossible for him to understand. Actually, he sees interpersonal relationships in terms of "conquest" because his life depends on "winning."

It makes sense for this person to operate according to the will-to-power. Since he thinks that he has control over everything, he need not be afraid of nothing. His mastery over the world and others gives him a certain sense of security. Moreover, he knows exactly where he stands, and since he controls the Other, the Other cannot threaten him. He gains a sense of solidarity and certainty in his willfulness, and often others initially give him a kind of affirmation. They admire his efficiency and objectivity or they may sense the strength in his ego willpower. From his frame of reference, his primary gain is to escape from no-thingness. He fulfills himself with things, and his control of everything prevents him from falling away into no-thingness. In fact, he does temporarily escape the pain, loneliness, and depression of no-thingness.

There are a number of individual reasons why a person escapes from no-thingness and displaces the Holy with power. A rather common reason is that a person's will-to-power is a reaction formation against his unconscious feelings of helplessness and inadequacy. He overcompensates for his weakness in facing himself and life. Since he has learned to reject his self and consequently has no faith in himself, he replaces the certitude of faith with the certainty of thinking. Often his sexual identity is tenuous, and consequently his interpersonal relationships are precarious. Since his life-style is a constant compensation for his repressed feelings of inadequacy, he is always forced to be certain of everything.

This person's mode of existence is a tragic self-deception, for his escape from no-thingness results in an escape from himself. He becomes more and more fragmented and alienated, and his efficiency slowly and progressively dissipates. While he is young, his ego strength is sufficient to adjust and be skillful, but in the crisis of his thirties he experiences his first vestiges of weakness not only in body but also in ego mind. With each crisis of no-thingness he becomes more and more threatened, and more and more compulsive to be in control. He begins to live in a state of panic. No-thingness—the one experience he cannot control—is always present.

He quickly loses the respect he once had from others; for others find him coldly obnoxious, and they begin to withdraw from him. He becomes lonely, bored, and disgusted. The very experiences he has tried to escape from are slowly catching up to him. He may try to escape into such activities as drinking or compulsive domination. But in time, no-thingness catches him, if not in the no-thingness of middle age, then in the crisis of old age. Finally, he has no-thing to control.

He finds himself in a bind because the only approaches he knows—control and manipulation—do not work. Thus, he fights himself in not accepting the experiences emergent from his no-thingness. Depression, loneliness, anxiety, and meaninglessness flood in on him. Since the power man has conditioned himself into rejecting no-thing, he gets caught in the chaos of no-thingness, and his dream of controlling everything leaves him as a no-thing.

Things lose their meaning and they no longer give

secure satisfaction. Self experiences are absent, and there is no transcendent meaning in life. Religious values are non-sense, and the Other is inaccessible. He is left in no-thingness with his crumbling ego, which is useless in regard to the mystery of no-thing.

Ultimately he is caught in the quagmire of a meaningless and groundless existence. He loses control, and life begins to overwhelm him. Since he cannot affirm his no-thingness, he cannot encounter the Holy; and the more he tries to control, the more he represses himself and the Other. In fact, the more he controls, the less control he eventually has. This person becomes a broken and lost man, for his will-to-power has left him will-less.

In the final analysis, this person is left with nothing but himself; since he has alienated himself from the Other, he lacks the ground of transcendence, and everything becomes boring. His displacement of the Holy into power has left him powerless and helpless to live meaningfully.

Although his situation is very difficult, this person is not hopeless. Sometimes this person experiences an involutional depression wherein he finds the opportunity to explore new horizons. He may come to accept his no-thingness and to be liberated from his compulsion to control things. Through his acceptance of no-thing he becomes free enough to direct his desire for the Holy to the Holy. He begins to own up to what he is instead of becoming something he is not. On the other hand, this person may never come to admit his no-thingness, so that he fails to confront the Other in his life and continues to lead a groundless existence. Instead of becoming a powerful god, he eventually ends up a helpless no-thing.

WORKISM

When work is the highest value in one's hierarchy of values, it serves as the central motivating force in a person's life and becomes "workism." Since work is primary and everything else is of secondary importance, life is seen in the light of work, not of love.

This person identifies his life with his work, and in Marcelian terms he becomes a "functional man." Since this person also operates primarily according to the ego processes, the work man is frequently and closely related to the power man. (The willpower person may also be a functional man by investing his willpower in his work.) Organization, planning, analyzing, thinking, coping, efficiency, and other ego processes are primary in this man's life; similar to the will-to-power man, he is devoid of self values. He uses his body in his work, but seldom enjoys his body, and he has no time for self and body experiences, for his life is his work.

However, this person is not as cold and efficiently barbaric as is the willpower man. He is a hard worker and often he is more flexible and more understanding, especially at work. In fact, people admire and resent him for his work and pity him for his life. The worker earnestly works himself to death without truly experiencing life.

The work person becomes so busy that life passes him by. He has no time to live, only time to work, and he eventually loses personal contact with the human and holy Other. For instance, he has no sense of re-creation. Play is a waste of time, and vacations are means of recuperating for work, not a way of vacating the routine life in order to be and to re-create. Or, he may work at playing, so that his compulsiveness to enjoy himself is a contradiction to the nature of play. Even in sexuality he works. If he takes the time, he uses techniques exclusively to gain maximum enjoyment. His entire life is task-oriented, and his work is a world of labor exclusive of the worlds of play, aesthetics, pleasure, love, etc.

Many people get caught in the bind of workism. For instance, a person who lives according to the values of having instead of those of being must necessarily work overtime because his life is based on possession, not on the Other and himself. He must make more and more money in order to have more, but he cannot afford to ask what his having is for. His possessions become ends in themselves, and yet he takes no time to enjoy them. In this situation, money is also made a displacement that is usually an attempt to hold on to things in order to escape from no-thingness. Money enables this person to run from life instead of serving him as a means of going deeper into life. Money becomes an end in itself and the most important end. In time, however, money becomes meaningless, and the person is left with no-thingness. This person slowly realizes that money does not help in no-thingness, life, and death.

Another example is the clergyman who identifies

his life with his work. His life centers around his profession instead of around his commitment to the Holy. Thus, when a church or a school is threatened with being closed, his own existence is threatened. He asks himself not only what he is going to do but also what he is going to be. The fact that he has made himself into a professional and is not a holy person is resented by many laymen. They begin to lose respect for the clergy and begin to feel that they are phonies. The clergyman often misinterprets this attitude and works even harder to prove himself to the world through work. Little does he realize that the layman wants him to be himself—primarily a holy person and secondarily a worker.

Life centered around work makes sense for many reasons. For instance, if a person has come from a poor environment or has lived through the throes of a depression, he may be overly anxious about possessions in order to gain some security and dignity. Or a person who compulsively keeps up with the Joneses may be trying to gain his sense of worth from having things instead of from within himself. Workism is also congruent with the culture that values a person's worth on the basis of his production rate. Furthermore, the pressure of contemporary living demands much money in that the cost to shelter, clothe, feed, and educate a family adequately is high. In short, the *Zeitgeist* is conducive to the work man.

Most important, work fulfills his no-thingness. Workism enables a person to escape temporarily from the unworkable pain of no-thingness. He need

not be anxious about no-things; work gives him a
bearing in life, something to hold on to, and results.
Work also helps to maintain him physically, eco-
nomically, and psychologically, so that after a good
day's work this person feels completed and satisfied.
He feels like somebody—like a good worker. Often
he is too tired to worry about no-thingness, for when
he works, eats, and sleeps, there is no time for no-
thingness. Work makes sense; no-thing is non-sense.
His work—not the Holy—gives him ultimate meaning in life. He becomes "a worker," not an authentic
man.

The work man's main crisis usually occurs in retirement because, since he has identified his life with
his work, the work man retires from life when he
retires from work. This person is left with what he
has conditioned himself to reject—no-thing. Initially
he searches frantically for work around his house,
but this work is not the same. Furthermore, his age
makes him limited, because the more he tries to
work, the more fatigued he becomes. Soon he is left
with time on his hands and he does not know what
to do with it; life becomes boring. Although his crisis of no-thingness is close, he still tries to escape
because he does not know how to accept it. The no-
thingness of death shakes the ground of his existence. He becomes progressively tired, bored, depressed, and lonely; and finally he is caught in
no-thingness.

Although it is possible for this person, especially
with support, to live through his no-thingness and
find life, it is more likely that he will die—psycho-

logically and prematurely biologically. Too often this person wants holy meaning in life, but he is unable to find the Holy in and through his no-thingness. He slowly wastes away, for his work displacement of the Holy has been taken away and he is frightened to death by the call of the Holy in no-thingness.

Although a woman may suffer more, she is usually more able to accept and to cope with this crisis of no-thingness. Since most women live a communal-centered life, they do not experience as sudden a change in life-style as do men. However, it is more difficult for a woman who is a professional person, because then the syndrome of experiences is similar to the man's. Indeed, the sudden and constant presence of a woman's husband changes her situation. Besides wondering what she is going to do with him, this woman also comes into a new way of living. Her children have grown and probably live somewhere other than with her so that suddenly she is left alone with her husband. If she has displaced the Holy with her work in the house and with her children, she too comes to a retirement crisis. If both parties have displaced the Other, they are left with themselves and they may discover that they have grown to be strangers to each other. If they refuse to accept the gift of the Other in no-thingness, life becomes worthless, and instead of seeing this as a time to love and enjoy each other, they grow more distant and die.

Work as the ultimate concern is doomed to dissipate, for work is basically a means toward greater ends. Thus, work is an inappropriate answer to man's yearning for the Other. Only the human and holy Other can give man's life, including his work, fundamental meaning and ground.

THEORISM

Theorism is another neologism used to refer to a rather common displacement, particularly for the person in his twenties and thirties. Theorism means that a person makes a system of thought or a particular theory his ultimate concern, so that he lives more in a theoretical world than in the experiential world. He sees his theory as being the main source of truth and tends to absolutize his theory to the exclusion of experience and other theories.

Theorism is primarily a function of the ego, because the ego is the level of theory construction. The theoretician reflects on experience and then tries to make sense of reality by means of his theory. His theory is an intellectual construction that approximates experience from a particular viewpoint. Although theories are necessary in order to comprehend explicitly the structure and functions of reality, an important point is that theory presupposes experience and should be in the service of experience. When a theory becomes a substitute for experience, the theory becomes theorism.

An advocate of theorism distorts or denies any experience that is not congruent with his theory. Instead of his theory being in service of experience, his experience is forced to be in service of his theory. This person lives primarily in his mind, not in his life. His theory becomes a displacement of the lived-world, including the holy experience. The kind of theorism that a person adopts is usually compensation for unsatisfied and unconscious needs. A needy person may choose from among several forms of theories, some of which will be discussed in the following paragraphs.

Psychology can be idolized and used to fulfill a person's no-thingness. Often some forms of psychology may seem more meaningful than forms of other sciences or of religion. Psychology particularly appeals to the person who has repressed his affective life, because psychology and psychotherapy may give him a needed opportunity to express himself. This person may see psychology as being more in harmony with his experience than other approaches to life. His psychological orientation gives him a sense of liberation from his past repressed life, and life seems to come alive through psychology really for the first time.

For instance, sensitivity training—a group dynamic approach—may liberate a person who has never really been in experiential touch with himself and with life in general. This group process can be excellent if it serves as an appropriate way to become in touch with life. However, it can be destructive if the group is not led by a qualified leader and if it is engaged in for the wrong reasons. Various forms of group process too often appeal to needy people who unconsciously see the group as a panacea for their personal problems or as a means for instant fulfillment. Or, too often people are forced to experience feelings for which they are not ready or for which they do not really choose. At other times, the group may turn into psychological and mutual masturbation. These groups can be greedily taken as a displacement of the Holy, particularly for the lost and unfulfilled person who is searching for significant meaning.

Another related danger is to play psychology games. A person begins to "psychologize" about life —every action has a psychological reason. Figuring out people gives him a decided advantage and a consequent sense of power and security. Psychologizing might also help him to justify any behavior for the sake of having the experience, behaving on the premises: if it feels right, it is right.

For this reason, psychology makes more sense than the Holy. Psychologism is made the ultimate value and central motive in his life. Psychology is not seen as a means of liberating man for an encounter with the Holy and with man. If another person does not fit into his psychological theory, the Other is rejected or made to feel guilty. The Other is sacrificed for the sake of psychology.

A person can also displace the Holy with a philosophical theory, stating that truth is found in philosophy, not in life. For instance, a philosophical system may give clear and distinct ideas of the Holy which give this person a false security in knowing exactly where he stands. His system may give him exact and clear standards for behavior, so that he does not have to worry about doubt, paradox, and crisis. Life is no longer a mystery. He knows everything and he need not bother with no-thing.

Too often his metaphysical notion of the Holy is

based on an antiquated philosophy that made sense centuries ago but does not necessarily make sense for contemporary experience. For example, he may give priority to conceptual instead of experiential knowledge of love, or he may see the Holy as the one who is always above man and consequently can be contacted only in solitude and not in and through man. Such a person may constantly "talk" about love of God and neighbor, but he seldom "lives" these commandments concretely in his day-to-day behavior. Since his philosophy primarily hides truth instead of revealing it, this person actually does a disservice to philosophy and to himself. Later in life this person finds it impossible to love a God of metaphysics. He discovers that his concept of the Holy is different from his experience of the Holy. He may even find that his love for his concept of the Holy was to some extent self idolatry (as criticized so well by the proponents of the "projection approach" toward God).

Actually, a person can adopt any theoretical system as a displacement of the Holy and therefore of life. Theology, psychology, sociology, anthropology, philosophy, etc., can be absolutized and lived as the ultimate concern in life. For instance, when a person considers that the only relevant truth comes from the positive sciences, he becomes an advocate of scientism. The scientistic person thinks that every experience eventually can be understood and controlled by the positive sciences. He analyzes the holy experience as a myth or a wish fulfillment that emerged in the past, unscientific times because of man's helplessness and insecurity. According to scientism, the person informed by science need not depend on God, but he can depend on science for the meaningful and ultimate ground of his existence. Thus, scientism displaces the Holy.

When a system of thinking is absolutized, the theory is perverted because its lifeline with experience is cut. The "logos" becomes an "ism."

All theories have truth and make sense. However, when "its" truth is made into "the" truth, the theory becomes theorism. The theory becomes the person's highest value, and experience takes second place. Since this person tends to meet others in terms of theory instead of meeting the concrete person, he never really engages the Other, although he may talk about dialogue constantly. In fact, this person becomes somewhat schizoid in becoming entrapped in his theory and cut off from experience.

A person who lives theory instead of life usually comes to his first great crisis in middle age. He was able to fulfill his no-thingness with theoretical truth in the past. He felt sure that he had "the truth," but his crisis of the limits throws him into no-thingness and forces him to see the limits of his theory. His experience in no-thingness appeals to him to look at the inadequacy of his theory in respect to life. He may feel that he has been out of touch with the lived world for a long time and he wonders how he can come back into life. In fact, it is common to observe a theoretician change his vested interest after he has gone through the crisis of the limits. For instance, the strict scientists begin to ask new questions, questions with a philosophical and a religious flavor, and the common man begins to look for the experiential God rather than for the theoretical God.

Although this person may be able to escape from no-thingness into theory even in the crisis of the limits, it becomes increasingly difficult to sustain a theoretical existence. Age tends to keep one honest. It is very rare to see old people playing theoretical games. It simply does not pay as it once did in the past. As always, no-thingness does catch up with the person. If a person has only theory to fall back on, he is left with the experience of no-thingness and he becomes helpless. His experience overwhelms his theory, and furthermore, he is tired of using theory. What good does theory do in death?

SEXUALISM

Sexualism is sexuality taken as one's ultimate concern. In this context, sexuality refers to one mode of sexuality—genital sex, actions that directly involve the genital organs and that directly lead to genital behavior. Although genital intercourse is the zenith of genital sexuality, other forms of sexuality, such as heavy petting, are also included in this discussion. Sexualism is a common displacement of the Holy, particularly in the second, third, and fourth decades of life.

A person who displaces the Holy with sex lives according to a sex principle: sex gives him ultimate satisfaction and meaning in life. Sex becomes his

central motivating force, and other values and be-
haviors are subordinate to it. This person works,
plays, and in general lives for sex, so that when he
is asked what he would most like to do, "Experience
sex" is his answer. All his actions are in some way
colored by his chief concern—achievement of sexual
pleasure. He is concerned for the Other insofar as
he can get sexual satisfaction. He lives a "playboy
philosophy," for he is indeed a boy who plays—plays
with himself and with others for his own pleasure.

This person lives primarily according to the sexual values of his body. He lives for the moment.
Since he wants gratification here and now, long-
ranged values are absent. He lives according to his
bodily desires and will use every means to satisfy
them. Suffering makes no sense to him, and as soon
as he experiences pain, such as the stress of no-
thingness, he escapes into sex. Values of the self are
not expedient, for they demand a respect for the
Other.

Both man and woman can become experts in the
"game of sex." A man might use his ego as a means
of achieving his sexual ends in knowing what to say
and when to say it. For instance, he learns that
many women are seduced by dependent honesty, need-
iness, and frustration, and he plays these roles. Or,
he may become an expert in being sensitive to lonely
women—women who will do anything for some kind
of comfort. The woman also plays the sexual game,
as when she learns how to present herself in an
erotic but safe way. She quickly learns how to ex-
cite the male, how to play with his guilt and re-

sponsibility, and how to make him think that he is
seducing her. It is often true that the man who
thinks he has "made" the woman discovers that he
was "made" sometime ago.

Men and women often play another kind of sexual
game that involves an implicit contract to satisfy
one another, and although the mutual agreement is
seldom overt, it is nevertheless real. The contract is
made on the basis of one's own satisfaction—not on
giving. They communicate to each other: if you satisfy me, then I'll satisfy you. Since a person as body
is centripetal, he takes without any notion of giving
for the Other's sake; thus, their sexual dialogue is
narcissistic.

Sexualism as a displacement for the Holy makes
sense primarily because a basic dynamic of sexuality is fulfillment. If a person is escaping from his
no-thingness and is necessarily looking for an ultimate concern, sex is a most accessible and fulfilling
displacement. Whether this sexualism is with another person or with oneself, it fulfills man's no-
thingness for several reasons.

Sexual fulfillment incorporates satisfaction. The
etymology of "satisfaction" indicates that the person is put at rest in sexuality. It takes away his
tension and makes him feel at peace. Sexuality also
offers a person a certain completeness in saying that
he has given himself. At the moment of sexual
climax, he experiences the completeness for which
he constantly searches; perhaps in no other way can
he find completion. A person feels that every fiber
in his being is activated. He feels whole. Sex makes

a lot of sense to a person who is leading a stressful and meaningless life, for in sex he can feel completely at ease without worrying about the throes of his life.

A person may be capable of being totally involved only in sex, and if he usually feels out of tune with life, sex can give him a feeling of being grounded. The lonely college sophomore may welcome sexuality as a meaningful relief from her no-thingness. Even though she may realize that her body is being exploited, she still feels that at least she is worth being used. The fulfilling contact of sex seems so much better to her than no-thingness.

Furthermore, it is pleasurable and fun to have one's body immersed in tingling eroticism. A person as body craves sex, for this is what he is—a sexual being, and his sex can finally let him "be" and have fun at the same time. A person in the crisis of the limits may also be tempted to fulfill his no-thingness with sex. He may be tempted to grasp something or someone rather than no-thing. This Don Juan can enjoy himself in the pleasure of sex rather than suffer in the pain of no-thingness.

The young adolescent who is experiencing negative no-thingness may also find sex a welcome relief. Here is something that makes sense and something that he can hold on to. Usually his sex centers on solitary masturbation where he can stimulate and gratify his new and strong erotic desires without the threatening limits of reality. He can be fearless and perfect in his sexual fantasy world without being scared and limited. Masturbation offers him unlimited possibilities to explore sexual reality, for he can do anything in fantasy. The Other never says no, because the Other does what it wants him to do. An older person may also masturbate, but usually for somewhat different reasons than those of the young adolescent. With an older person, the decision to masturbate usually emerges from a "non-sexual" situation. His masturbation is not linked to the satisfaction of newly found genital drives, but is frequently an escape from the pain of no-thingness.

Furthermore, a person's immediate and prereflective pleasure means that he does not have to think, but can let himself go. A person who primarily lives from the neck up (theorism) may find the immediacy of sex a therapeutic experience, for he can come out of his theoretical world into the experiential world. He does not have to experience the world through the rubrics of technology, science, or language, but can experience it prereflectively. He can retreat from an abstract world of complex mediation to a concrete world of simple immediacy.

A person also experiences power in sexuality—the power of ecstasy, the quiet power of being fulfilled and completed, the strength in being able to let go of oneself, and the potential power of creation are all present. When a person's power is not a spontaneous consequence of loving sex, his power is selfishly turned inward and becomes narcissistic. For example, a solitary masturbator has power in creating his fantasy world wherein he is the most powerful sexual being. Or a person may feel power in his ability "to make" the other. The man feels power in penetrating and satisfying the woman, and the woman feels powerful in being able to make the male become helpless in her arms.

Furthermore, too many men use their power in sexuality as a means of compensating for their inadequate sexual identity and fear of women. In their sexual exploits they feel powerful in being on top of the woman. Likewise, the woman's envy of man because of his control of the world is compensated for by her seduction and exploitation of the man. Therefore, both man and woman can gain a sense of power in different ways. In both cases, however, the striving for power in sex is usually a compensation for inferiority feelings toward one's own sex and toward the opposite sex.

A person also experiences a certain kind of ecstasy or quasi transcendence in sexuality. He literally goes out to and into the Other. A person who is out of his mind, in that he is not living his life, experiences sex as a pleasant return to life; he begins to experience himself by going out of himself. This person also experiences ecstasy in that he is away from the routine of everyday life. Sex has no room for the tensions of everyday living, and it transcends normal time and place. The genital encounter is experienced as a timeless affair.

Sex also transcends the dichotomy between pleasure and pain, between joy and suffering. For instance, the partner's sounds in sex often attest to this unique and concrete paradox, at least insofar as it is difficult to distinguish between joy and suffering in the sexual climax. In a certain sense a

person comes close to death in his climax and at the
same time he feels most alive. He has spent himself
and yet he feels most himself.

Particularly in its initial encounters, sex has an
almost unique relation to the holy experience. Its
quasi transcendence closely approximates the transcendence of a self experience. The immediate fulfillment, completion, and actualization of sexuality
give meaning to a person's life. In this sense, sex
is a quasi satisfaction of the transcendent movement of love. Nevertheless, even though a person in
sexualism may initially try to love in some way, his
love is not committed, long-lasting, and inclusive
activity. Without love, his somatic and functional
levels operate exclusively, and his genitality becomes
a substitute for love and therefore of the Holy. A
person's fulfillment in sexualism is temporary and
inadequate because his sexuality needs the vitaliza-
tion and support of love to make it last; otherwise,
sexuality soon dissipates into onanistic behavior.
Since the satisfaction of sex without love does not
last, a person must go back for more and more; he
becomes a sex addict.

A person who indulges in sexualism is selfish in
that he unconsciously and/or consciously exploits
the Other. His sexualism is not a concrete communication of love, not an affirmation and promotion of
the Other. Neither does his behavior incorporate the
world, but it is exclusive of it. Genital sex without
love is an "inverse ratio" of the sexual fulfillment
experienced in love. His sexualism becomes all-
exclusive as contrasted to the all-inclusive fulfillment

in loving sex. Sex without love makes "a world" the world; thus, it is selfish, not reality or Other-centered. Like the infant, this persons wants, takes, depends on, and sucks off the Other. Thus, body-sex without self love becomes an inadequate fulfillment of no-thingness.

A significant aspect of sexuality is that its structure and function are creative and concrete. In promoting and leading to transcendence, fulfillment, and completion, genital sex calls for love and therefore commitment and responsibility. Consequently, in genital sex without love, a person makes an implied promise that is never fulfilled. This occurs because the nature of genital sex points to more than itself—to the promise of loving genital fulfillment. If a person does not keep his promise, frustration and often consequent anger result. The woman especially feels this frustration, for it is her initial propensity to seek love and creation in sexuality. Furthermore, genital sex takes time and space, so that genital sex outside marriage simply becomes unwieldy. An unmarried person is forced to scheme as to how he will manage his sex encounters. Thus, authentic sexuality is the unity of transcendency, space, and time that calls for a reliable situation of commitment and responsibility. This situation is generally called marriage. Conversely, genital sex without love is irresponsible and masturbatory.

A person who displaces love with sex is constantly searching for new bodies and thrills to satisfy his desires. His fixation on the immediacy of sex forces him to find different bodies. He unconsciously searches for the transcendent love in his exploits, but his futile attempts never find what he really needs, because he asks sex to be the Holy.

If this sexualistic person does not run around from body to body or even if he does maintain his sex fixation, his sex orientation will eventually dissipate. Time and age prove decisive, so that the older the person becomes, the less he can rely on sex. He has less energy, is less attractive, has less desire, and love calls him. It becomes increasingly difficult to satisfy himself through sex, and his search for the meaning of life in sex leaves him lifeless.

Sexualism means that a person's body, which he is, is made the ultimate. However, since man's body is peripheral and temporary in its satisfaction, sex in itself is not enough. Only the Holy can satisfy man's need for the Holy. Although sex may lead to love, love—not sex—leads man to the Holy.

Parenthetically, alcoholism and drug addiction are very similar to sexualism as displacements of the Holy. Alcohol is a popular and socially sanctioned escape from the loneliness of no-thingness and is particularly seductive for the dependent person. Like sex, alcohol offers the seduction of immediate pleasure and a temporary and selfish sense of well-being. While under the influence of alcohol, a person does not worry about the demands of his no-thingness and about the meaninglessness of his existence.

The drug addict also goes on his problem-free trip. Getting and taking drugs become his ultimate concern, and everything and everyone is of secondary importance in reference to drugs. The drug addict feels few or no qualms even in exploiting his loved ones to get a "fix." Other forms of drug usage, such as LSD, offer an instant escape frequently from personal and cultural theories. LSD enables a person to break out of the bondage of ego processes and to plunge himself into the primacy of the body. Like sex, alcohol and drugs offer temporary and inadequate fulfillments of no-thingness.

LOVISM

Although love is the primary way to the human and holy Other, love can be used as a displacement of the Holy. "Lovism" means that a person displaces his desire for the Holy with an exclusive desire for man. Since lovism includes a denial of the Holy, a person's love becomes inauthentic.

A follower of lovism considers the Holy to be an interpersonal relationship, that is, love between humans exclusively. "God is love" means that love equals God, so that when two people love each other their love equals the Holy. In this orientation, life after death may be considered to be the person's heritage that he leaves on earth primarily through love; thus, he lives forever through his love acts.

Others may say that the Holy is social interest. Being the opposite of willpower, social interest incorporates an unconditional concern for one's fellowman. When man reaches a perfect state of social interest he has then become the Holy. The Holy may also be considered as a symbol of man's state of perfection, so that the Holy is man when he achieves the nirvana-like state of self-actualization.

The advocate of lovism usually functions primarily on the self level. He tries to live a life of love and tends to be highly critical of non-self values such as technology and everyday living. He is ultrasensitive to self and non-self experiences, and he spontaneously differentiates between them. Honesty, authenticity, encounter, commitment, love, freedom, etc., are paramount in his world; simple sincerity and presence is his way of living. Structure, establishment, inauthenticity, solitude, etc., are words that are frowned upon.

Love as a displacement for the Holy is a very subtle deception, for the argument—God is love and love is God—contains much truth. However, this viewpoint is only partially correct.

We have already seen that love, the most perfect of human experiences, actualizes man and is the wellspring of wholeness and holiness. In love a person promotes the happiness and goodness of the Other for the Other's sake, and he becomes more of himself by giving himself in love. He discovers that the meaningful order of love is an adequate answer to the meaningless chaos of no-thingness. In and through love he finds the ground for a meaningful and actualizing life. In love life makes sense. On the other hand, we saw in Chapter 2 that love is an interpersonal relationship which should be oriented to man and to the Holy. Since authentic love includes both man and the Holy, the exclusion of one eventually destroys the other. A person must love the Holy implicitly or explicitly in his love of man, but he must also be open for the holy encounter in solitude. The crucial point is that exclusive love of man is not a substitute for the love of the Holy. In fact, a denial of the personal transcendent in love with man or in solitude perverts man and displaces the Holy.

The addict of lovism tends to live in a fantasy world in thinking that love is a panacea for everything. He may even try to love constantly, which is an impossible accomplishment, for man is not merely a loving being. Consequently this person will fall apart or be extremely tired under the tension of love. This person must realize that his body and ego are also valid and necessary modes of behavior and that his love must be implemented via his body and ego.

Love exclusive of the Holy, however, does make sense. Love movements, for instance, are often reactions against the inhuman behavior of the culture or of one's own environment. Often subcultural groups are formed in order to practice the way of love without the inhumanness of the overall culture. Although participation in these groups can be a step in development, if promoted too long, these groups tend to drift off into fantasy; that is, they have few ties with the common world. They forget that love must be implemented in the everyday, concrete world for it to be authentic. Whether the world is phony or not, it is still the real world. Otherwise, their love becomes exclusive, which is contrary to the nature of love. Dependent persons are prone to join these love groups, for like the child, they need others to exist; consequently, they give love in order to receive love. Often they are still searching for the love they received or should have received as children. They depend too much on man and not enough on themselves and the Holy.

A person in lovism may also fall into a subtle form of masochism or sadism. The masochistic lover feels that he can get fulfillment from another person only by losing himself. He is willing to give himself to another at any cost, but his giving is for his own sake instead of for the Other. Since his meaning in life depends on other people, not on himself, his life is out of his control. Or, a person who must always be in control of his love may become a sadistic lover. He cannot let go of himself, nor can he receive from the Other. Sometimes he falls into the "Jesus Christ syndrome" wherein he roams around giving love and blessings to those not so fortunate as he—usually to those weaker persons who depend on him. The masochist's love gives him a humble feeling of mammary satisfaction, and the sadist's love gives him a proud sense of virile security.

Other persons of lovism may be reacting against "solism" wherein a person can experience the Holy only in solitude. Thus, solism is the opposite of lovism in that the solistic person rejects the Holy in his love encounters with people. In contrast to the advocate of lovism, this solistic person will eventually have to take a stand toward the Holy in his human relationships. If he opts to reject the presence of the Holy in interhuman relationships, his explicit love of the Holy in solitude will disintegrate.

The celibate mode of living particularly lends itself to this solistic displacement of the Holy. In this situation, instead of liberating a person for man and the Holy, celibacy is used as a means of withdrawal from the Other. The potential freedom of celibacy is perverted into a narcissistic escape from no-thingness. Living in his schizoid holy world, this schizoid celibate does not have to be concerned about the dynamics—the limits and potentials—of human relationships. On the other hand, some people react against this solistic approach and fall into lovism. For instance, a celibate woman, especially in her thirties, may see marriage as the only way for fulfillment. Marriage seductively offers her the convenient but temporary escape from the loneliness of no-thingness, and the new benefits of sex, children, and constant companionship are fulfilling. However, she fails to realize that if she cannot find herself in celibacy, she will probably be worse off in marriage. In some ways, a celibate person has to be healthier and holier than a married person, for a celibate lacks the immediate and gratifying benefits of marriage. However, since it is not so easy for a celibate to escape from no-thingness, the celibate can have a better opportunity to confront the Holy in and through no-thingness.

If a person in lovism does not reject the Holy, his lovism in its early stages can be an immature but authentic response to no-thingness. For instance, it may be temporarily meaningful for a young adult to rebel against his inhuman view of God. If he has been taught about God merely in "supernaturalistic" terms, he may go to the opposite extreme and try to encounter God merely in "naturalistic" ways. He may see God only in human relationships exclusive of solitude. This humanism not only may be more meaningful than his past abstractionism, but it may eventually lead to more mature love—love that explicitly incorporates both the human and holy Other.

A humanist who lives in love without the explicit promotion of the Holy will usually come to a crisis. He will have to opt for or against the Holy. If he opts to be closed to the Holy, his love for his fellow-man will slowly dissipate; if he opts to be open to the Holy, his love for man will grow. Thus, the humanist's love can be a preparation for direct love of the Holy while being a temporarily fulfilling and an adequate answer to his no-thingness. However, if a person rejects the Holy, he will eventually get caught in the chaos of no-thingness, for only love of man and the Holy can save man from his no-thingness.

RELIGIONISM

The disciple of "religionism" tries to displace the Holy with inauthentic religion. Religionism can be the most subtle and dangerous displacement of the Holy, for it is done in the name of the Holy.

The religionistic person lives according to a set system of religious behavior, and consequently follows a special form of theorism. He knows the exercises for being religious, but he lives the rule instead of living the holy life. This person develops a safe and powerful way of living, for it seems that he always knows the right way. There is no room for ambiguity and mystery. He eschews his self experiences of the Holy in favor of ego functions and experiences. He thinks, plans, and decides his religious life. He even thinks that he can tell other people exactly what to do in order to be holy. In converting or helping another, this person uses his ego motives of domination instead of his self motives of appeal.

We contend that rules, standards, and laws are necessary and have much value; but rules are fundamentally for life, not vice versa. These constructions of the ego make sense only when they are rooted in and are reflections of experiences. Rules should be incitive, not prescriptive. Rules do not tell a person exactly what to do, but they shed light and point the way. Instead of his religious values and standards being rooted in experience, the advocate of religionism blindly submits to external rules, so that he is childish as a religious person.

A main reason for this legalistic dependency is that early in life a child is conditioned to follow certain "shoulds" and "should nots." He is too young and dependent to explore the world himself, and, more fundamentally, he has not reached the age of responsible freedom. However, too many adults carry these conditioned standards throughout life, and they try to live according to childish standards that are incongruent with their experience. Most of the standards are given to man by his culture primarily through his parents. Although these inherited standards are usually and basically true for the child and his parents, the young adult must make them his own. The first positive experience of no-thingness brings a crisis of identity that leads to a reevaluation of these standards. This person asks what is truth for him, and he rebels against blind submission to his past standards. He asks: How can I live my standards? How can my central motivation for living come from within? How can I become a person of conviction and commitment instead of a person of submission? The late adolescent wants to live his life and become a true adult.

This person may find that his standards and experiences are not in harmony, and he seeks to find a way to have his standards promote life instead of repressing it. We have seen that he begins to doubt everything in the service of no-thing. He lives the experiences of no-thingness, and it threatens many adults around him. Seldom is he given support, permission, and guidance to accept his no-thingness, and he may be made to feel guilty for his doubt of religion. Through this pressure and his own inability to accept his situation, he may be seduced into accepting a "ready-made" religion, and consequently displace the Holy with religionism. This person now experiences the safety and power of religionism, and he enjoys the support and affirmation of the religionistic group—those people around him who also play the game of being holy. He becomes proud in knowing that he can look down on people in the name of the Holy, and yet he wonders why others resent him. In smug holiness he prays for them.

This person becomes a caricature of a holy person. Although he goes through all the motions, people know that he is acting. Slowly he becomes a hollow shell—rigid and brittle—so that when the voice of the Holy speaks to him in no-thingness, he may crumble. Those things—rules, standards, and laws— will no longer speak to him, but he is called to speak to things. He may not know that he must vitalize the rules, and that the rules will not vitalize him. If a person finds the Holy, man, and himself through no-thingness, then he will emerge to a mode of living wherein his standards are rooted within himself and in harmony with his unique personality. They will promote life, love, and encounter with the human and holy Other. His religious system will be a lived system. Otherwise, both his system and he will be lifeless.

SUMMARY

Our proposal has been that man displaces the Holy in order to fulfill his no-thingness. Through his displacements man tries to make sense of life and to be someone. He strives to find a ground for his existence—to find existential meaning in life. Theoretically, any object or activity can replace the Holy and be an inadequate response to man's yearning for the Holy. Furthermore, if a person tries to displace the Holy with a substitute object, he will eventually alienate himself from his fellowman and from himself.

We conclude that love is the ground of man's being—love for and from man and the Holy. The Other is man's hope of finding meaning in life, and man must have faith to experience the human and holy Other. His experience of the Other saves him from his no-thingness, and this saving grace is love for and from the Other.

5
Healthiness and Holiness

WHAT IS HEALTHINESS? What is holiness? Are
they the same? If not, how do they differ? What are
their interrelations? In the light of our previous dis-
cussions and by way of summary, we respond to
these issues.

A HEALTHY PERSON

One key feature of a healthy person is that he actualizes himself and the Other to the fullest possible
degree without the impediments of psychological
pathology and existential displacement. He realizes
and maintains an ongoing harmony of his three
modes of existence. His body, ego, and self are vi-
tally integrated and not at odds with each other.
Knowing that all his modes of existence are necessary and meaningful interactions with reality, he
does not sacrifice one system for the other. According to the situation, a healthy person behaves in a
way that is appropriate to his situation. For instance, if ego interaction is called for, he does not

love explicitly, or if play is appropriate, he does not act in a task-oriented manner.

A healthy person, however, can never actualize all his potentiality, mainly because of structural, constitutional, cultural, and environmental factors. Since a person grows in degrees of healthiness, a child, for instance, cannot be as healthy as an adult. Or, identical twins may have the same genetic endowment, but because of their different environments the actualization of their potential may differ significantly. However, both persons may be healthy in that they actualized themselves in their situations— although in different ways and to various degrees. Our main point is that a healthy person is open to his experience of reality if and when it is possible.

A healthy person promotes an availability to his body functions in listening to, accepting, admitting, and integrating the knowledge of his body. He is in tune with his own "expression" and is sensitive to the expression of the Other. Since a healthy person values and is present to the prereflective world of his body, sexuality is important to him; he values being a man or a woman. He lacks a schizoid or puritanical denial of his and others' bodies and of the body at large—the world. Feelings, moods, and body interaction in general are an essential part of his humanity. A healthy person, furthermore, affirms his limits and admits that he is a being-toward-death. He also grows and becomes sensitive through his suffering.

A healthy person functions in his ego mode when a situation elicits this behavior. He can usually work more fully and efficiently than the normal person.

He does not have to be preoccupied with other things besides his job; he is free to work. A healthy person is also realistic in that he is open to reality and in that he learns how to implement his ideas. His ego strength enables him to take charge of a situation and to distance himself from being seduced by trivia or from losing balance in sentimentality. Through his ego functions, he can communicate logically, explicitly, and publicly. Since his ego processes are oriented not only toward the world but also toward himself, he is able to integrate feelings, thoughts, and experiences. Finally, a healthy person as ego reflects on his prereflective body and self experiences and makes explicit sense of life.

The self dimension is the core of a healthy person's motivative system. He becomes himself and discovers the Other in and through his no-thingness. He does not displace the Other, but he opts for a ready availability to and for reality, and since he freely determines himself, he becomes the author of his existence. This person is committed and has fundamental meaning in life, and his existence is grounded in love. In time, since he grows in openness, this person becomes wise and childlike. Although he promotes his body and ego, his self experiences and values are most important to him. Love, understanding, acceptance, compassion, insight, responsibility, freedom, spontaneity, zest for life, etc., betray his healthiness. A healthy person becomes more and more of himself by giving himself in love to the Other. He realizes that he can actualize himself only by trying to actualize the Other.

A healthy person is happy and good. Since he lives

in harmony or at peace with himself and others, happiness permeates his existence. He is basically happy even when he confronts personal problems or conflicts because he owns up to what he is experiencing. A healthy person is also a good man in that he promotes the emergence of life. His body, ego, and self, love and celebrate life.

Whereas a healthy person grows into openness and out of closedness, an unhealthy person moves into closedness and out of openness. This person opts to be closed to certain experiences. For instance, a person who represses his self dimension in spite of the opportunity to actualize his self would be an unhealthy person, or a person who represses his emotional life would be attempting to disown what he is—an affective person. Since he is forced to lead a defensive and cautious life, an unhealthy person uses much time and energy to frustrate the dynamic openness of his self. He is compelled to develop and repeat processes that repress, deny, and distort his unacceptable experiences. Furthermore, an unhealthy person is repeatedly compelled to use the Other to gratify his unsatisfied needs.

Unhealthiness is usually not a matter of willfulness or of free option, but is due most often to pre-reflective dynamics of which a person is unaware. Nevertheless, such a person pays the price for not letting himself be. He experiences unhealthy anxiety, depression, restriction, somatic illness, tension, etc. His existence becomes a lived contradiction. He must be constantly careful not to let himself be.

Most people are neither healthy nor unhealthy,

but they try to lead a normal life of adequacy. Adequacy means to be barely sufficient, to satisfy the minimum demands of life. The normal person leads an adequate life in that he is able to meet the minimum demands of his life. However, this person does not actualize the Other and himself to the fullest possible degree, nor does he live an orientation of love. He does just enough to maintain his life, particularly in the area of self functions. This value of "just enough" is a symptomatic sign of the normal person and its implementation—the coping mechanism of just enough—enables him to prevent mental illness.

The etymology of adequacy indicates that a person who lives an orientation of adequacy tries to equalize his needs to a state of gratification. In Freudian parlance, this person strives for a comfortable state of equilibrium. For example, when a normal person experiences so-called signs of unhealthiness such as anxiety, depression, and tension, he immediately judges "it" as something to be gotten rid of by means of psychic or somatic repression. Since he fails to realize that these feelings are a manifestation of himself instead of an "it" to get rid of, he seldom accepts and understands himself in his feelings.

Normal people live an adequate life to various degrees and for various reasons. Some people's primary concern is adequacy and their marginal existences are testimonies to their fundamental inadequacy. Others may lead adequate lives by investing too much energy in one realm and by which they displace the Holy. Still others move in and out of adequacy and frequently regress to adequacy when under stress. Some people realize that their lives are actually inadequate and they try to transcend their normalcy. Some succeed in their transcendence, but others never quite make it.

The reasons for a normal, adequate existence are many. Some immature persons never have had the opportunity to lead lives other than adequate ones. Furthermore, cultural and environmental forces often promote adequate modes of living. For instance, such strong cultural values as having rather than being, need gratification, technocracy, and the repression of self experiences often promote adequacy. An adequate life can also be combined with unhealthiness, particularly neurosis, in that unconscious forces compel a person to live normally and unhealthily. Another person may willfully opt to live the adequate life so that he gratifies himself at the expense of others.

R. D. Laing, a British psychiatrist who writes about the madness of normal people, is quite helpful in this context. Laing states that most people live out of their minds, that is, not in tune with their experiential lives. Since these people make up the majority of the population, this "formation" is usually presupposed to be authentic; but Laing questions the healthiness of this normal formation, pointing out that it may be a procrustean quagmire that incorporates a massive devastation of experience. He says that although these normal people are not ill in the traditional sense, they can be considered to be mad, for they are estranged from the most important experiences—those of authentic love, commitment, freedom, and openness. In short, this normal formation does not necessarily include the right way. Thus, a person who desires to live the way of authenticity must be somewhat out of the majority formation and consequently abnormal. (*The Politics of Experience*, pp. 81–82.)

The important point for this analysis is that a life of adequacy is normal but also mad, because it basically precludes a ready availability for and promotion of life-emergence—including myself and the Other. To do just enough, to satisfy the minimum demands of life is a form of madness. Although a normal person submissively or unconsciously falls into the formation of the mad majority, a healthy person freely opts to live in formation. He realizes that actualization of himself and the Other necessitates that he enter into the world of normal formation. He knows that normalcy is also a dimension of his reality. However, a healthy person also opts to go out of formation in order to find his way and yet he maintains a ready availability to implement his concerns in the formation of normalcy. Another kind of abnormal person—the holy person—is our next subject of discussion.

A HOLY PERSON

Although a description of the holy person has already been given in Chapter 2, particularly in terms of the consequent positive changes of the holy experience, the analysis did not include the con-

structs of no-thingness and displacement. For the
sake of coherency and for its summary value, a suc-
cinct account of the holy person is presented and
then used in comparing the holy and healthy persons.

We have seen that a holy person lives according to
the values and demands of the Holy. Since the Other
in love is the holy person's ultimate concern, his
central motivation is love. And although only a small
part of his total life involves direct love-encounters
with the Other, all his behavior is permeated with a
holy orientation. A holy person's body and ego behavior disclose the Holy, and his self experiences,
especially those of love, proclaim the Holy. Thus,
every action is in some way in service of the Holy.

Since a holy person promotes experiences of the
Holy, his experiences of the world and others incorporate the numinous, the paradoxical, and the mysterious. He does not identify a person with his function, talent, or possessions, but he incorporates what
a person is with what he can be. His faith and hope
open him to the mystery of transcendence of the
Other. His deeper penetration into reality lets him
see the holy orientation of other persons even though
they may be leading a displaced life.

Since a holy person lives in an orientation of holiness, he speaks of the Holy. He is not constantly and
explicitly preaching the message of the Holy, but
neither is he embarrassed to speak of the Holy when
it is appropriate. A holy person is not scared and
ashamed to talk of the very reality he stands for.
When a situation calls for explicit discourse on the
Holy, he has the courage to speak the Holy even

though he may be socially rejected. On the other hand, he never stops speaking the Holy in implicit but very present terms, for his behavior is a radiation of the Holy.

The paramount sign of a holy person is love. He structures his life so that he can take time to love the Holy in solitude and with others. He is careful not to get caught in such displacements as workism so that he has little time for the Holy. In fact, all his activities are second in priority in regard to the Holy. Since his life is highly influenced by his transcendence in love to a sacred Other, he is not likely to be seduced by the profane, but he celebrates the profane in the light of love.

A holy person's life is also marked with existential indebtedness, guilt, worship, faith, and doubt. He is aware of his indebtedness to the human and holy Other, and his gratitude to the Other is expressed primarily in concrete manifestations of love. Besides enabling him to be constantly restless and unsatisfied (and yet he is at peace with these feelings), his existential guilt pushes him to grow into holiness. A holy person also takes time to worship in solitude and with others. Realizing the importance of his holy encounters, he worships with a certain humility and pride. His authentic worship sets him aside from the normal mode of living, yet he dares to be abnormal in standing up for the Holy. Finally, faith and doubt permeate his existence. He creatively accepts and celebrates the numinous and he welcomes doubt as an opportunity to go deeper into the Holy.

A holy person tends to be charismatic. His charisma does not necessarily mean that he has a dynamic personality, but that his holy orientation attracts and inspires people. People sense the presence of the Holy in him and they are inclined to listen to him. Others spontaneously want to know more about him as is shown in their respect for him.

Since a holy person lives in an orientation of love, he necessarily promotes life. A holy person does not harm or do violence to his fellowmen, but he sees his fellowmen as brothers who are oriented toward each other and toward the Holy. A holy person tries to do what is best for the Other and is willing to suffer for the Other's sake. He becomes a good person by doing good to others, and consequently he is moral. When the laws of morality are personalized they become a matter of inner conviction. Even though the holy person leads a good life, he is aware of the demon that lurks within him, and he openly affirms that his humanity includes the possibility of doing evil. By accepting and saying no to his evil inclinations, he grows more in goodness and farther away from evil.

Finally, a holy person leads a meaningful life. He grows in and out of his no-thingness to a progressively deeper celebration of things, and he discovers not only himself in no-thingness but also the Other. He does not displace the Other with substitute objects, but opts for the Holy as the ground of his existence. His love for and from the human and holy Other saves him from his no-thingness and enables him to find his place in life. Since his holy experiences are functions of his self, a holy person is inclined to have other self experiences such as wonder, beauty, and compassion. Although his life makes sense, a holy person is not necessarily happy, for happiness involves being in basic harmony with oneself and the Other, and a person need not be in harmony in order to be holy. A holy person may be in unhealthy conflict because of factors that he cannot possibly cope with. This relation—healthiness and holiness—is the final topic of discussion.

A HEALTHY AND HOLY PERSON

Psychological health and holiness are related but are not identical. Since both healthy and holy persons live in love, they have ground and meaning in their existences. Love for and from the human and holy Other gives them meaning for being. Both persons also accept their no-thingness and actualize their self modes of existence. Neither of them displaces the Other, but through their no-thingness they come to find their place in being with the Other. Thus, both the healthy and the holy person emerge out of no-thingness into a life that is motivated mainly by their self. However, there are differences between them.

First, consider the healthy person in relation to holiness. It is quite possible to be healthy without direct worship of the Holy in that a person loves his fellowman but has not yet come to an explicit love of the Holy. Thus, this person loves the Holy implicitly in and through his relationships with man. If the Holy is not directly present to a healthy person, he finds himself in a state of not-yetness. His not-yetness means that he experiences an implicit presence to the Holy, but not yet an explicit one. Although healthy, this person is somewhat immature in regard to his holiness.

Because of his orientation of openness and love, this healthy person will usually come to a confrontation with the Holy—to opt to accept or reject the Holy. The critical factor is that a healthy person does not reject the Holy or displace the Holy with a substitute object. If displacement does occur, then this person is no longer healthy or whole, for he represses part of himself—his orientation toward the Other. If he opts to reject the Holy, he will become unhealthy, and if he opts to accept the Holy, he will begin to promote explicit holy encounters along with his implicit ones. This person becomes a healthy and holy person.

Parenthetically, many people opt neither for nor against the Holy, but they try to lead a marginal existence with the Holy. They consider the Holy as one experience among many—not an experience of special and sacred import. These persons try to opt for the Holy especially in times of need, but tend to displace the Holy in times of plenty. These people maintain a normal relationship with the Holy.

Holiness, however, is no guarantee for healthiness. A person may be holy but unhealthy. Many holy people are far from being models of mental health, yet they are good and holy people. A holy person may be unable to be open to or to integrate certain experiences because of past fixations, traumas, or repressions. For example, a holy person may be unable to admit his feelings of hostility. Although this holy person experiences the Holy, he is closed to his hostility. This holy and unhealthy person does not willfully reject his experiences, but because of unconscious processes his freedom to opt for openness is curtailed. This person leads a holy and good life, but not necessarily a happy one.

On the other hand, a person's holiness may help him to endure and even make sense of his pathological pain. His love orientation enables him to accept his experiences, including the pathological. Thus, this holy person is less likely to fight or repress his unhealthiness, but is more likely to transcend it. He finds deeper meaning in his suffering. This holy and unhealthy person is basically happy, for he lives with and transcends his suffering.

Nevertheless, holiness is not a magical panacea for unhealthiness. Although unhealthy functions do not preclude holy experiences, they may impede a fuller experience of the Holy. Since a holy and unhealthy person is closed to dimensions of his experiences, he cannot fully involve himself. In a sense, he is less than he could be when he presents himself to the Holy. Thus, a holy person should strive for psychological health, for it increases his availability to and for the Other. Holiness promotes wholeness, as does wholeness promote holiness. A holy person's availability to the Holy promotes openness to all his experiences, and a healthy person will be open in all areas.

A paramount point is that holiness is not synonymous with healthiness. A catchy phrase—"Holiness is wholeness"—can be just as atheistic as it is humanistic. Or, the phrase, "Divinization is humanization," can put the reality of God totally in the hands (personalities?) of men. People who live according to these assumptions tend to make healthiness their ultimate concern. Here, healthiness is a displacement for holiness. When a person makes healthiness his main value in life, he is likely to become too concerned in solving all his personal problems. He is inclined to focus too much on himself and not enough on the Other. When healthiness becomes man's ultimate concern, life can become too easily an exercise in madness. Holiness is much more within man's grasp precisely because it is beyond his grasp. The hope of mankind lies in holiness, not in healthiness.

The ideal is to be holy and healthy. This person is open to and functions appropriately in all his modes of existence. His ultimate concern is love for and from man and the Holy. Out of no-thingness and through love he finds and becomes himself, and he brings love to the world and the world to love. This authentic person has the freedom and courage to be out of normal formation and the commitment to celebrate his abnormal concerns. Through his life of love, he becomes (w)hol(l)y.

Selected Bibliography

Allport, Gordon W., *The Individual and His Religion.* The Macmillan Company, 1950.

Barth, Karl, *God Here and Now,* tr. by Paul M. van Buren. Harper & Row, Publishers, Inc., 1964.

Berdyaev, Nicolas, *The Divine and the Human.* London: Geoffrey Bles, Ltd., 1949.

Berger, Peter L., *The Sacred Canopy.* Doubleday & Company, Inc., 1967.

Boisen, A. T., *The Exploration of the Inner World.* Harper & Brothers, 1936.

Brothers, Joan, *Readings in the Sociology of Religion.* Pergamon Press, Inc., 1967.

Buber, Martin, *I and Thou,* tr. by Ronald Gregor Smith. 2d ed. Charles Scribner's Sons, 1958.

De Lubac, Henri, *The Discovery of God.* P. J. Kenedy & Sons, Publishers, 1960.

Eliade, M., *The Sacred and the Profane.* Harper Torch Books, 1959.

Feuerbach, Ludwig, *The Essence of Christianity,* tr. by George Eliot. Harper & Brothers, 1957.

Frankl, Viktor E., *The Doctor and the Soul: An In-*

troduction to Logotherapy. Alfred A. Knopf, Inc., 1955.

Freud, Sigmund, *Civilization and Its Discontents,* ed. and tr. by James Strachey. W. W. Norton & Company, Inc., 1961.

————, *The Future of an Illusion.* Doubleday & Company, Inc., Anchor Books, 1964.

Goldbrunner, Josef, *Holiness Is Wholeness and Other Essays.* University of Notre Dame Press, 1964.

Heidegger, Martin, *Being and Time,* tr. by John Macquarrie and Edward Robinson. Harper & Brothers, 1962.

Heschel, Abraham J., *Who Is Man?* Stanford University Press, 1965.

Hocking, William Ernest, *The Meaning of God in Human Experience.* Yale University Press, 1912.

James, William, *The Varieties of Religious Experience.* The New American Library, Mentor Books, 1958.

Jaspers, Karl, and Bultmann, Rudolf, *Myth and Christianity.* The Noonday Press, 1958.

Jung, C. G., *Modern Man in Search of a Soul,* tr. by C. F. Baynes. Harcourt, Brace & World, Inc., Harvest Books, 1955.

————, *The Undiscovered Self,* tr. by R. F. C. Hull. The New American Library, Mentor Books, 1959.

————, *Psychology and Religion: West and East,* tr. by R. F. C. Hull. Pantheon Books, Inc., 1958.

Jurji, Edward J., *The Phenomenology of Religion.* The Westminster Press, 1963.

Küng, Hans, *The Unknown God?* Sheed & Ward, Inc., 1966.

Kwant, Remy C., *Encounter*, tr. by Robert C. Adolfe. Duquesne University Press, 1960.

Laing, R. D., *Politics of Experience*. Pantheon Books, Inc., 1967.

Lepp, Ignace, *Atheism in Our Time*. The Macmillan Company, 1963.

Luckmann, Thomas, *The Invisible Religion*. The Macmillan Company, 1967.

Luijpen, William A., *Phenomenology and Atheism*. Duquesne University Press, 1964.

——, *Existential Phenomenology*, tr. by Henry J. Koren. Duquesne University Press, 1960.

Marcel, Gabriel, *Problematic Man*. Herder and Herder, Inc., 1967.

Maslow, A. H., *Toward a Psychology of Being*. D. Van Nostrand Company, Inc., 1962.

——, *Religion, Values, and Peak-Experiences*. Ohio State University Press, 1964.

Moore, Thomas Verner, *The Life of Man with God*. Doubleday & Company, Inc., Image Books, 1962.

Moustakas, Clark, *Loneliness*. Prentice-Hall, Inc., Spectrum Books, 1961.

Mowrer, O. Hobart, *The Crisis in Psychiatry and Religion*. D. Van Nostrand Company, Inc., 1961.

O'Dea, Thomas F., *The Sociology of Religion*. Prentice-Hall, Inc., 1966.

Otto, Rudolf, *The Idea of the Holy*. Oxford University Press, Galaxy Books, 1958.

——, *Mysticism East and West*. Collier Books, 1960.

Padovano, Anthony T., *The Estranged God*. Sheed & Ward, Inc., 1966.

Pahnke, Walter N., and Richards, William A., "Implications of LSD and the Experience of Mysticism," *Journal of Religion and Health,* Vol. V., No. 3 (July, 1966), pp. 175–188.

Rahner, Karl, *The Christian Commitment,* tr. by Cecily Hastings. Sheed & Ward, Inc., 1963.

Robinson, John A. T., *Honest to God.* The Westminster Press, 1963.

Rümke, H. D., *The Psychology of Unbelief.* Sheed & Ward, Inc., Canterbury Books, 1962.

Salinger, J. D., *The Catcher in the Rye.* Little, Brown and Company, 1945.

Sartre, Jean-Paul, *Being and Nothingness,* tr. by Hazel E. Barnes. Philosophical Lib., Inc., 1956.

Scheler, Max, *Man's Place in Nature,* tr. by Hans Meyerhoff. The Noonday Press, 1961.

Schleiermacher, Friedrich, *The Christian Faith,* Vol. I. Harper & Row, Publishers, Inc., 1963.

Teilhard de Chardin, Pierre, *The Divine Milieu.* Harper & Row, Publishers, Inc., 1960.

Thouless, Robert H., *An Introduction to the Psychology of Religion.* London: Cambridge University Press, 1961.

Tillich, Paul, *Dynamics of Faith.* Harper Torchbooks, 1957.

———, *The Courage to Be.* Yale University Press, 1952.

Underhill, Evelyn, *Mysticism: A Study in the Nature and Development of Man's Spiritual Consciousness.* E. P. Dutton & Company, Inc., 1911.

———, *Practical Mysticism.* E. P. Dutton & Company, Inc., 1915.

————, *The Mystics of the Church*. Schocken Books, Inc., 1964.

Van Croonenburg, Bert, *Gateway to Reality*. Duquesne University Press, 1965.

Van der Leeuw, G., *Religion in Essence and Manifestation*. 2 vols. Harper & Row, Publishers, Inc., 1963.

Van Kaam, Adrian, *Religion and Personality*. Prentice-Hall, Inc., 1964.

————, *Existential Foundations of Psychology*. Duquesne University Press, 1966.

Wach, Joachim, *Types of Religious Experience, Christian and Non-Christian*. The University of Chicago Press, 1951.

Wallace, Anthony F. C., *Religion: An Anthropological View*. Random House, Inc., 1966.

Watts, Alan W., *Nature, Man and Woman*. The New American Library, 1960.

Weber, Max, *The Sociology of Religion*. Beacon Press, Inc., 1964.

Webster's Third New International Dictionary. G. & C. Merriam Company, Publishers, 1961.

Weigel, Gustave, *The Modern God*. The Macmillan Company, 1959.

Weil, Simone, *Waiting for God*, tr. by Emma Craufurd. G. P. Putnam's Sons, 1951.

White, Victor, O. P., *God and the Unconscious*. The World Publishing Company, 1952.

Whitehead, Alfred North, *His Reflections on Man and Nature*, ed. by Ruth Nanda Anshen. Harper & Brothers, 1961.